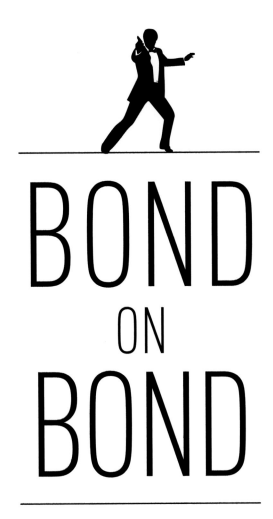

BOND
ON
BOND

For every copy of this book sold in the
UK, a royalty will be donated
to UNICEF UK
(registered charity no. 1072612)

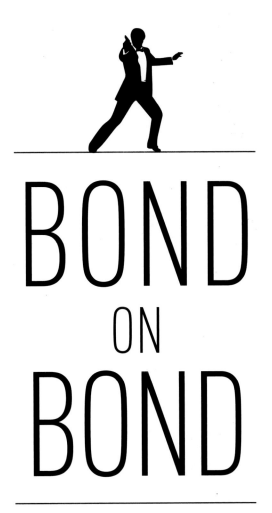

BOND
ON
BOND

The Ultimate Book on 50 Years of Bond Movies

ROGER MOORE

with Gareth Owen

Michael O'Mara Books Limited

For my favourite Bond girl – Kristina

First published in Great Britain in 2012 by
Michael O'Mara Books Limited
9 Lion Yard
Tremadoc Road
London SW4 7NQ

A CIP catalogue record for this book is available from the British Library.

Papers used by Michael O'Mara Books Limited are natural,
recyclable products made from wood grown in sustainable forests.
The manufacturing processes conform to the environmental regulations
of the country of origin.

ISBN: 978-1-84317-861-3 in hardback print format
ISBN: 978-1-84317-885-9 in EPub format
ISBN: 978-1-84317-914-6 in Mobipocket format

1 2 3 4 5 6 7 8 9 10

Designed and typeset by Design 23

Printed and bound in China

www.mombooks.com

CONTENTS

INTRODUCTION

The year 2012 not only witnesses the release of the twenty-third James Bond film in the shape of *Skyfall*, but it also marks fifty years since our intrepid hero first burst onto cinema screens in *Dr. No*.

We've seen six incarnations of Jim Bond – whose name his creator Ian Fleming borrowed from the author of a book entitled *Birds of the West Indies* – in the official Eon-produced series of films: Sean Connery, George Lazenby, Timothy Dalton, Pierce Brosnan, Daniel Craig and ... erm ... oh yes, me!

It has been suggested that over half the world's population

BELOW: The scene in which the infamous line, 'Bond, James Bond', is first delivered by Sean in *Dr. No*.

has seen at least one of the films in what has become the world's longest-running movie franchise; and a series in which 007 has got to know over fifty-five 'Bond girls', has fought over 130 villains and *femme fatales*, has knocked-back numerous vodka martinis, has driven five different models of Aston Martin, has visited over fifty different countries and has been armed with over one hundred gadgets and guns – a few of which he even returned intact.

The escapism, entertainment, fun, beauty and thrills that so encapsulate each and every film were set down by the blueprint designed by producers Albert R. 'Cubby' Broccoli and Harry Saltzman, who helmed the early movies together before Cubby took the reins alone in 1977; which he in turn then handed over to his daughter Barbara and stepson Michael in 1995.

The combined box office of the first twenty-two films has exceeded $5 billion and while the *Harry Potter* and *Star Wars*

ABOVE: *Goldfinger* was the first Bond film to have a premiere, which was held at the Odeon Leicester Square. The crowds went crazy and had to be held back by the police.

ABOVE: *Octopussy* proved to be another crowd puller.

films may come close, they have enjoyed more limited theatrical life spans whereas Bond is very much set to continue indefinitely and – who knows – maybe he too will even get a 3D retro-makeover?

It isn't just about cinema, either. I'm often told by people, friends and fans, how they regarded it as a big occasion when a Bond film first came on TV, in the dark ages before DVDs and online streaming, that is, and I'm proud to say that when, on Christmas Day in 1980, *The Man With The Golden Gun* premiered, it attracted (and has since held the record of) the largest ever audience of any Bond film on the box. In fact all the 007 films, not just mine, regularly attracted huge audiences on broadcast, which, incidentally, the networks usually reserved for Bank Holidays and Christmas. Coupled with those screenings, the wide and affordable introduction of VHS (remember that?)

and DVD opened up an even bigger market for the films, and brought with them new audiences to the continuing franchise.

There is certainly a huge loyalty in the world of 007 fans; fans who not only collect the films, but also the memorabilia, the books (such as this one, dear reader) and posters; they also anticipate news of upcoming adventures, with huge excitement, on the multitude of fan sites and forums in which they scrutinise, analyze and dissect every little detail. Of course, many on these forums insist I'm their favourite Bond, but modesty prevents me complimenting their amazingly good taste!

Although 2012 marks a golden anniversary for the series, it also marks a ruby anniversary for me. You see, in October 1972 I reported for duty as the third actor to play James Bond on screen for Eon Productions. Can it really be forty years ago? Back then I could leap out of a chair without fear of my knees cracking; could chew on a toffee without fear of losing a filling, or worse still a tooth; could admire my long flowing locks of hair; and as I swooned in front of the mirror, proudly admire my bronzed, slim torso. Ah yes, with a flex of my toned muscles and a twitch of the old eyebrow I set pulses racing across the world, they say.

These days it's my pacemaker that keeps my pulse racing and as for my other above mentioned attributes … well, I still have my memories.

When I was invited by my publisher to take a look at the Bond films from my own fairly unique perspective (well, unique in that there are only six of us) of being James Bond on the big screen, it seemed rather a taxing demand for someone who has only appeared in seven of the films, and who is not necessarily an avid repeat viewer of the others. However, by calling on a few friendships and with the guidance of one or two people, I have attempted to fill up the spaces between some lovely photos with interesting words, thoughts and memories. What I can't remember, I'll just have to make up.

BELOW: A typical day in the Moore household. It's a hard life, but someone's got to do it.

BOND

ON

BEGINNINGS

BOND ON BEGINNINGS

As I write I am sitting in Monte Carlo with my wife Kristina. The sweltering sun is beating down upon us as we sip our early-morning coffee, slip on our dark glasses and watch the millionaires – and billionaires – passing by in their designer clothes, their fast cars and on their yachts, while their luscious lady friends, all potential Bond girls, are busy sunning themselves on the terraces at the Monte Carlo Beach Club. It is a very 'Bondian' setting in which to write a book, though I feel I should start by confessing it wasn't until 1962 that I first heard mention of James Bond – some eight or nine years after Ian Fleming had started writing his hugely popular books – but they, and he, had somehow passed me by.

PREVIOUS PAGES: Bonded by success: Harry Saltzman (right), Ian Fleming and Cubby Broccoli pose for a photo after signing their agreement to produce the first James Bond film in 1962.

LEFT: The birth of an icon: a very early publicity shot of Sean Connery as 007.

WILL HE, WON'T HE?

Following a spell in Hollywood, where two studio contracts were swiftly followed by a plane ticket home, in 1960 I wound up in Rome, making a couple of what you might call 'miracle-movies'. That is to say, it was a miracle if anyone got to see them.

My agent, Dennis Van Thal, called while I was in Venice gorging my face on a favourite dish of black pasta, flavoured with a little garlic, shallots and with a decent handful of prosciutto, all complemented by a glass of Pinot Grigio on the terrace of the Gritti Palace Hotel, which itself sits on the banks of the picturesque Grand Canal. Very Flemingesque, eh?

Dennis had received an offer from British television mogul Lew Grade for me to play Simon Templar in a television series of *The Saint*. I was immediately and greatly interested because I knew those books and had, in fact, at one point made an – unsuccessful – approach to their author, Leslie Charteris, to buy the rights.

To cut a long story short, I accepted the contract and found myself back in England with a regular salary jingling away in my pocket.

A little financial security is always a good thing for an insecure actor, and with it I soon began behaving in a Bond-like fashion by

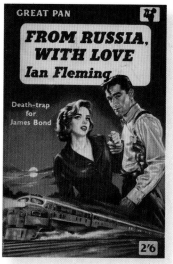

ABOVE: It had to start somewhere! A few covers of Ian Fleming's books, which I'm assured all sell for more than 2 shillings and 6 pence these days. Interesting that I'm on the cover of *Dr. No* – even though a well known Scottish actor was in the film.

visiting the tables of the gaming houses in London's Curzon Street. It was there I first met two larger-than-life, and obviously affluent, American gentlemen who introduced themselves as producers Harry Saltzman (a Canadian) and Cubby Broccoli (an American of Italian descent). Over the ensuing months we exchanged a fair amount of casino money across the table, but moreover developed a close friendship, which lasted the rest of their lives.

They were then just setting out on producing a series of films about 'James Bond'. That was the very first time I'd heard the name.

RIGHT: Photocall on the roof of London's Dorchester Hotel, announcing me as the new James Bond with director Guy Hamilton on the left, Cubby Broccoli in the middle and Harry Saltzman on the right. Note how Harry's looking at my hair, wondering how many inches I should lose.

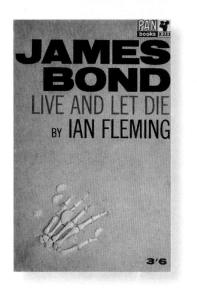
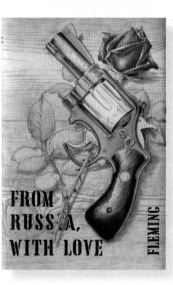

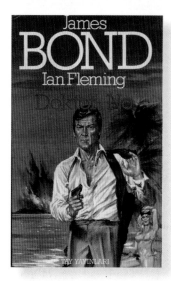

Cubby and Harry told me about agent 007 and invited me to the first screening of *Dr. No* and, later, all the other Sean Connery Bond films, at their Mayfair headquarters, Eon Productions in South Audley Street. I was greatly enlightened, entertained and captivated by the good Commander and his amazing exploits.

The Saint, meanwhile, happily ran and ran. In fact I clocked up 118 episodes over seven years. It was towards the end of the penultimate series in 1967–8 that the idea of me playing Jimmy Bond was first mooted. Sean Connery had completed *You Only*

BELOW: I was big in Birmingham. A ticket stub for a first-night screening.

ABOVE: With my dear friend Lew Grade, who told me that playing Bond would ruin my career.

RIGHT: I was expected to do everything! On location for *The Man With The Golden Gun.*

Live Twice and stated that it was to be his last. Keen to keep the franchise afloat, the producers started thinking about recasting. They must have heard I worked cheap.

Producer Harry Saltzman called. 'Let's talk about you doing Bond.'

Producers, writers and agents' discussions commenced around an adventure set in Cambodia. Unfortunately, very soon afterwards all hell broke loose in that country and the production was shelved. With uncertainty about what might happen, and with the prospect of another – financially appealing – series of *The Saint* looming, I returned to film what would be my last season of the show.

Keen to get back into movies, I simultaneously began developing a couple of projects with my *Saint* producing partner Bob Baker, one of which – *Crossplot* – we filmed with funding from United Artists, the backers of the Bond movies. I then became an actor-for-hire

ABOVE: Here I am at the premiere of *Live And Let Die* with my benevolent producers.

in *The Man Who Haunted Himself* for Bryan Forbes at EMI, before teaming up with Bob Baker again to star in, occasionally direct, and produce a TV series called *The Persuaders!*. Oh, and thanks to my friendship with Cary Grant I also took up an executive position at Brut Films to oversee a few rather successful productions, including the Oscar-winning *A Touch Of Class*.

Life was pretty good, and very busy. Cubby and Harry were busy doing their thing too, and while we stayed in touch, when they regrouped I became 'unavailable' due to my own filming commitments, and so they made Jimmy Bond an Australian, albeit for one adventure only.

Only after Sean returned for – and said 'never again' following – *Diamonds Are Forever*, in 1971, was I brought back into the frame and, happily, I was between acting gigs.

'Are you alone?' Harry asked when he called me long distance at my Denham home (my phone number, oddly enough, was Denham 2007). 'You mustn't talk about this,' he added, 'but Cubby agrees with my thinking in terms of you for the next Bond.'

I didn't say anything to anyone. Once bitten, twice shy.

Contracts were drawn up and duly signed. It was a few weeks before Harry called again, to say he and Cubby felt I was 'too fat' and my hair was 'too long'. I said I'd get a haircut and take the weight off.

I told my dear friend Lew Grade (who along with *The Saint* also bankrolled *The Persuaders!*) that I was to be the next 007. With tears welling in his eyes, he shook his head and said, 'Roger, don't do it. It'll ruin your career!'

'What career?' I hear you say.

There is always a huge challenge associated with taking over a role from another actor, particularly when he has enjoyed great success in said role. I knew I'd face comparisons and wondered if I'd even be accepted by audiences. However, I consoled myself by thinking about the hundreds of actors who have all played Hamlet. Besides, if it didn't work out I could always go back to modelling sweaters and gorging myself on more Flemingesque lunches in Venice, while letting my hair grow down my back.

BELOW: It's not every day my getting a haircut made the newspapers.

SQUARE CUT

For 007, the old 'short back and sides' is a must

Studio barber giving Moore the treatment

By IAN CHRISTIE

THERE is more to being James Bond than just signing a fat contract, thwarting the villains and accepting the advances of ravishing girls. In a sense it is like joining the Army.

For Roger Moore, who takes over the role in the next Bond adventure, "Live And Let Die," was given the order by producer Harry Saltzman: "Get your hair cut!"

Agent

was not the approved hair-style.

Said Harry Saltzman: "After all, he is not just a civilian, he is Commander Bond."

Image

Co-producer Cubby Broccoli commented: "We think Bond looks more masculine with his hair cut to a reasonable length.

"This is the image we have built up over the years and it is one we wish to keep. Basically Bond is a square."

FINDING THE KEY

At the outset, I knew I would have to be tougher than the other screen heroes I had played: Beau Maverick, Ivanhoe, Simon Templar and Brett Sinclair. However, having known many soldiers and servicemen, I didn't necessarily believe that Bond was a man who enjoyed killing. He'd have to be rather sadistic to get a kick out of it. In fact, when I re-read the Fleming novels there was a line that stated, 'Bond did not particularly enjoy killing'. And that was the key to my interpretation of the role: I wouldn't enjoy killing, but I'd do it professionally, quickly and accurately.

What else? Well, Fleming made it clear Bond enjoyed the finer things in life from food, drink, cars and travel to, ahem, women. That's not a bad job description, is it?

But what of Bond the man? Ian Fleming gave very little away about the character until he penned an obituary for Bond. Had the author not been persuaded otherwise by his publisher, the obituary would have come a lot sooner than it actually did. After just four books, feeling he'd done his duty and his adventures had run their course, Fleming grew tired of his hero, much as Arthur Conan Doyle had done with Sherlock Holmes. He fully intended to have Bond murdered at the end of *From Russia With Love*. Thankfully, he was talked out of it and continued the series. The memorial piece was reserved until *You Only Live Twice* was published (six novels later) – and was written by 007's boss, M.

'Commander James Bond, CMG, RNVR,' it started, referring to Bond's naval service and his being a Companion in the Order of St Michael and St George, 'was born to Andrew Bond, of Glencoe, Scotland, and Monique Delacroix, from the Canton de Vaud, in south west Switzerland.'

Andrew Bond was a foreign representative of the Vickers armaments firm, and Jimmy travelled with his parents wherever their work took them. When Jimmy was but a mere eleven years of age, both parents were killed in a climbing accident in the Aiguilles Rouges, France.

Jimmy was an orphan. Poor Jimmy.

Bond's early education was undertaken abroad and so he became fluent in both French and German. After his parents' deaths, young Jim went to live with his aunt, Miss Charmian Bond, in Pett Bottom, a hamlet near Canterbury, Kent.

Then, Fleming revealed, aged twelve our young hero was entered at Eton College, but after a year there was 'some alleged trouble with one of the boys' maids' and he was transferred to Fettes College in Edinburgh, where he took part in wrestling, founded a judo class and graduated early at the age of seventeen.

As for me, at seventeen I'd left school, been fired from my first

BELOW: Having lost some hair, I was now trying to get fit and lose some weight – at my family home in Denham.

job (not through problems with any maids, I might add) and was wondering what I would do with my future. Unlike Jimmy, I was not recruited by the special branch of the Royal Navy Volunteer Reserve, nor, a few years later, was I approached by MI6.

Thankfully, the obituary was a ruse to put off Jimmy's pursuers. He wasn't dead, but it proved a helpful ploy in the adventure. It also proved helpful to us readers in stitching together a backcloth to the character. I've never been guilty of method acting – or even acting, if you want to argue a point – but doing this bit of background reading in *You Only Live Twice* gave me a few ideas about the character and why he was who he was. But throughout I kept thinking about that line 'James Bond did not particularly enjoy killing'. That was the key.

BRITISH NAVAL COMMANDER MURDERED

In the early hours of this morning, in an Hong Kong Hotel bedroom, was discovered the body of the British Naval Commander James Bond.

The body was discovered by two Police Inspectors of the Hong Kong Police Force, who answered an emergency call from a nearby bar. The gunfire was heard by people in the street below, and the police were on the scene within minutes.

As yet there has been no arrest made, but the police are working on a definite clue. Foul play is suspected and the question is being asked what a high ranking naval officer was doing in such a notorious district.

ABOVE: Bond's demise was reported in *You Only Live Twice* on the front page of a newspaper.

THE BOND PHENOMENON

Sean Connery had enjoyed huge success as the first filmic Bond. When *Dr. No* first hit the screens in 1962, in my humble opinion, where leading heroic parts were concerned, Sean changed everything. The world of Bond blew a hurricane breath of fresh air into the adventure-movie genre with its larger-than-life villains, even more evil than Satan himself; drop-dead-gorgeous girls who in fact did often drop dead if they found their way to Bond's bed in the first half-hour of the film; hugely glamorous locations and sets; and a hero who was impeccably turned out, with the best taste in everything and the enviable ability to disrobe a leading lady in the flick of a camera shutter.

In an era when travel was the reserve of the rich, post-war rationing and rebuilding was still a vivid memory, and fine living

ABOVE: Although relatively few details are known about Jimmy's home life, he did have a driving licence for one of the films. Westminster? Hmmm. I thought he lived in Chelsea.

consisted of a night out at the pictures followed by a fish-and-chip supper, James Bond offered something exciting – something previously unimaginable. Bond swiftly became a phenomenon.

But, as with all success stories, it very nearly wasn't.

Harry Saltzman had an option on the books, which was fast running out. Columbia Pictures had turned it down, as had other potential backers. It was through partnering with Cubby Broccoli, and Cubby's friendship with Arthur Krim at United Artists, that the series was eventually launched.

A deal was struck with Krim and the fact that Cubby was able to loan Harry the airfare to get to New York and sign the deal saw the making not only of a great franchise, but also of a brilliant Scottish actor's career, as well as fairly regular employment not only for Bonds but the villainous characters, glamorous girls, extras willing to fall off bridges and stuntmen keen to be hurled into the air by explosions and dive into shark-infested pools. The screenplay was co-written by Richard Maibaum, who went on to collaborate on twelve more of Jim's adventures.

It is well documented that the first James Bond film was given a $1 million budget – and even for 1962, that was considered tight. Thankfully, it increased exponentially film by film, not least to accommodate my fee …The future of the franchise was very squarely dropped at my feet in 1972. I was to be the first English actor to play 007, and quite possibly the last if I ballsed it up.

THE SAME, BUT DIFFERENT …

So how do you follow someone as hugely popular as Sean? I hear you ask. Well, I was conscious I should at least not speak with a Scottish accent, and after discussions with director Guy Hamilton it was decided I would never order a vodka Martini, neither shaken nor stirred, nor would I drive an Aston Martin. They were too closely associated with Sean. I had to be the same, but different.

Of course, I watched Sean's films again, and while not speaking directly with him about the part – after all, would I have called Larry Olivier and asked him about playing Hamlet had I been offered it? – being a friend of his I knew why he quit the role, and remember his declaring he'd 'created a monster'. Sean wanted to distance himself from 007 and the associated hysteria and potential typecasting, to tackle other acting roles. I, on the other hand, was just grateful for a job.

Oh, and I should not forget George Lazenby, who had one shot at playing Jim in *On Her Majesty's Secret Service* in 1969. By his own admission George was not an actor. He was a car salesman who began modelling and then slid sideways into acting work. His good looks and ability to throw a punch, coupled with his arrogance, secured him the part. I got to know him later on and, with hindsight, he admitted he had made a huge mistake in not signing on for seven movies, as originally offered, and parachuting out after just one on the advice of his friend-cum-manager Ronan O'Rahilly, who stated, 'Bond is Connery's gig. Make one and get out.' The irony is, George is probably never going to be able to shake Bond off.

My friend Peter Hunt directed *On Her Majesty's Secret Service* and, while very pleased with how it turned out, did confide in me that he'd had many problems with his lead actor's behaviour; presumably not helped by Harry Saltzman saying, 'You are now a star, George. Behave like one.' Stories became legendary of George sending back the studio car in the mornings because he didn't like the colour, demanding a car to take him the fifty yards from his dressing room to the Pinewood restaurant, and of eating garlic ahead of a love scene.

As had become the tradition, Cubby and Harry invited me to Eon's HQ in South Audley Street to watch the first screening of *On Her Majesty's Secret Service*. I guess there were thirty or forty other people there, one being Bob Goldstein, who then headed up 20th Century Fox. He stood up at the end of the film, leaned over to Cubby and said in his gruff voice, 'You should have killed him and saved the girl!'

In October 1972, I picked up my script, turned to page one and, heeding the advice of The Master, Noël Coward, prepared to 'learn the lines and don't bump into the furniture'. I guess I did something right, as, from then until we wrapped on my seventh Bond adventure thirteen years later, people went to see the films and kept me gainfully employed.

When I handed in my licence to kill I was constantly asked who should replace me. No! I lie. I was asked that question after about my third film, which, of course, gives an insecure actor a great feeling of being wanted. In fact, I did make a number of suggestions to Cubby – always names of really bad actors so I looked good by comparison. In the end, I was forced to abandon that idea as I couldn't find any actors worse than me.

BELOW: Ready for action in *Live And Let Die*, my first outing as Jimmy Bond.

ALBERT R. 'CUBBY' BROCCOLI CBE

I could write a whole book on Cubby alone. He was a big man in both life and charm. A kind, caring and fun person, Cubby would always listen to ideas and suggestions from any member of the crew – he might not necessarily agree, but he listened – and that was a quality that endeared him to everyone. He was known universally as Cubby, from studio heads to the tea lady. There were no pretentions or nasty sides to Cubby. Sure, he could be tough in business, but his heart was a big one and his loyalty unswerving.

Cubby had read Ian Fleming's books and thought they would make terrific films, but on enquiring about the rights discovered that a Canadian producer named Harry Saltzman had an option on them, which is how the duo got together in the first place. From there, a production company named Eon was formed, and the rest is history.

Cubby's enthusiasm for Bond never diminished. He loved making the films, and took great pride in showing every dollar of the budget up on the big screen. But that was never enough for the press: they always asked Cubby if he ever wished he'd won an Oscar.

'The only award I need is green with Washington's head on it,' he replied, referring, of course, to dollar bills at the box office. A successful movie was bigger than any trophy to Cubby. However, in 1982 the issue was addressed by the American Academy, when they bestowed their highest honour – the Irving G. Thalberg Award – on my friend. They asked me to present it to him on the night, and I remember Dana, his wonderful wife, looking rather worried that I might say something silly and fool around on this very prestigious night. Me? Would I?

After *Octopussy*, I resigned myself to thoughts of retirement. There are only so many stunts an ageing actor can tackle, and only so many young girls he can kiss without looking like a perverted

grandfather. However, I was persuaded back by Cubby for *A View To A Kill*. A year later and with rumours of a new Bond script being finalized, I decided I really couldn't go on to an eighth. I sat down with Cubby, who had obviously had similar thoughts, and it really became a mutual decision over lunch that I would step down. There were no tantrums, no attempted negotiations. It was all extremely amicable.

My friendship with Cubby outlived my time as Bond, and he told me of his thoughts of casting Pierce Brosnan in the role of 007. I said it was a terrific idea, as Pierce was an actor not unlike myself in style and looks. When that didn't quite work out because of contractual complications, Cubby told me he was signing Timothy Dalton for three films, and I wished them both great success.

The next time I met up with Pierce and Timothy was in 1995, at the memorial service for Cubby at London's Odeon Leicester Square. When I last saw him in California we laughed and joked about the times we'd shared, but, alas, Cubby was suffering ill health and was never able to return to the set of a Bond film, which I know he so looked forward to doing. I miss him greatly.

BOND
ON
VILLAINS

BOND ON VILLAINS

PREVIOUS PAGES: Evil Hugo
Drax with manservant Chang
in *Moonraker*. Although
French, Drax did so enjoy
taking afternoon tea in his
château.

They're a jolly bunch of people, all loved by their mothers and all with a sick plan to take over the world or dominate it in one form or another. From the feared head and members of SPECTRE to international drug barons, deadly assassins, warped idealists and terrorists ... from the sublime to the ridiculous and back. They are all Bond villains.

In truth, I always wanted to play a Bond villain as they invariably have the best dialogue – describing their complex, evil and very sinister schemes to do away with Jimmy Bond – whereas 007 just walks around saying his name and ordering Martinis. The villains aren't on set every day, either, which means I'd have had a few days off here and there!

OPPOSITE LEFT: It all started
with Dr. No, as played by
Joseph Wiseman. I wouldn't
advise you to shake hands
with him, as he has cold
hands *and* a cold heart.

BELOW: Get a grip, man!
Dr. No's metal hands couldn't
do much to save his slippery
descent into hell.

THE SPECTRE OF EVIL

In several of the books and early films it is the aforementioned SPECTRE – the **SP**ecial **E**xecutive for **C**ounter-intelligence, **T**errorism, **R**evenge and **E**xtortion – with which Jimmy is most concerned. Its evil head, Ernst Stavro Blofeld, is not aligned to any nation or political ideology, aside from his own unhinged ones.

SPECTRE arose from the need to create a politically neutral enemy for Bond. In 1959, with the Cold War at its height, Ian Fleming, Jack Whittingham and Kevin McClory were writing a screenplay on which the novel *Thunderball* was later based. However, Fleming thought that the Cold War could end in the two years it would take to produce the film, which would make the film feel like 'old news' even before release. So they decided instead to create SPECTRE, the dastardly twenty-one members of which are drawn from six of the world's greatest criminal organizations – the Gestapo, the Russian counter-intelligence agency SMERSH, President Tito's legendary secret police, the Mafia, Corsican

hoodlums from the Unione Corse, and a Turkish drug-smuggling operation.

SPECTRE's main aim is to spark conflict between the superpowers – the Soviet Union and the United States – in the hope that this conflict will make them vulnerable enough for SPECTRE to snatch their power. In *From Russia With Love*, Blofeld likens SPECTRE's *modus operandi* to the three Siamese fighting fish he keeps in an aquarium, noting how one fish refrains from attacking the other two until their fight is first concluded. Then, the waiting fish attacks the weakened victor and kills it much more easily.

But it was not all plain sailing for SPECTRE, as it and its characters became the centre of long and bitter litigation between Kevin McClory and Ian Fleming. When plans were abandoned to film the story written by Fleming, McClory and Whittingham, Fleming later published it as the novel *Thunderball*. A court case ensued and, in 1963, Fleming settled out of court with McClory. However, McClory secured the film rights to *Thunderball*, although literary rights remained with Fleming.

After the 1963 settlement, Eon Productions made a separate agreement with McClory to adapt *Thunderball* into the fourth official James Bond film, while stipulating that McClory would not be allowed to make further adaptations for at least ten years – perhaps thinking that by then 007 would have run out of steam? After several failed attempts to re-make *Thunderball*, in 1983 McClory finally succeeded to produce *Never Say Never Again*.

Never one to leave the stage quietly, McClory later contested the filmic ownership of James Bond himself, and threatened to make other 007 films based on earlier script ideas he'd penned. After another court case, in 2001 the UK courts awarded Eon Productions the exclusive film rights to the character James Bond. However, until his death in 2006, McClory continued to claim that SPECTRE and its evil head were his inventions – even launching a legal action when he heard that Karl Stromberg was to be a member of SPECTRE in *The Spy Who Loved Me*. The use of the organization was avoided by Eon from then on.

THE CHANGING FACE OF BLOFELD

Super-villain Blofeld first featured on screen – albeit not in camera shot – in *From Russia With Love*, although identified by name only in the closing credits of the film. Anthony Dawson supplied his body, Eric Pohlmann his voice. The gimmick was repeated in *Thunderball* but when *You Only Live Twice* commenced filming, Jim was to meet Blofeld in person. At last, we were going to see him!

Czech actor Jan Werich was cast as SPECTRE's 'Number 1' but both producer Cubby Broccoli and director Lewis Gilbert were anxious when he arrived at Pinewood at the start of the shoot, feeling that Werich resembled a 'poor, benevolent Santa Claus' rather than an arch villain. Lewis started filming but within a few days it became apparent

ABOVE: Jan Werich filmed only a few scenes as Blofeld in *You Only Live Twice* before departing the production ...

LEFT: ... in favour of the more menacing Donald Pleasence.

31

ABOVE: But in *On Her Majesty's Secret Service* Blofeld had another look, and came in the shape of Telly Savalas.

that Werich simply wasn't menacing enough. So they recast the role with Donald Pleasence.

'They had already started work on the film,' Donald Pleasence revealed, 'and the Blofeld character was still open. They said they wanted me to read the script and create a character totally different to anything that had been done before, and I think we achieved that.'

He experimented for about a week at Pinewood with humps, lame hands and a beard – not all at once, mind you – before it was decided the now-distinctive scar would best convey the character's almost Himmler-esque quality of villainy (and, as Donald played Himmler on film, that was a good analogy of mine, I reckon). Thus one of the screen's most memorable villains was born.

On the swift re-casting, actor Burt Kwouk, who played SPECTRE's 'Number 3' in the movie recalled, 'One day we were filming with Werich in the control booth, and then the next day I turned around and there was a different actor sitting in Blofeld's chair.'

Whoever was in Blofeld's chair, one somewhat unexpected – and unfortunate – occurrence came as a result of all the explosions on set: Blofeld's trademark white Persian cat didn't take too well to them, and frequently relieved itself on its master!

Two years later, in *On Her Majesty's Secret Service*, the feared head of SPECTRE returned in the guise of Telly Savalas. Given there was much more physicality involved in this movie – including skiing – director Peter Hunt didn't feel the more diminutive Pleasence would be convincing as an athletic Blofeld. So he turned to Greek-born Savalas. Blofeld escapes – as he does in earlier films – but not before he and his sidekick Irma Bunt murder Bond's new bride, Tracy. Understandably, Jim sets out on revenge and, in *Diamonds Are Forever*, tracks down his old nemesis – this time played by Charles Gray.

When George Lazenby was cast as 007, and thoughts were turned to introducing the different-looking character, Cubby had a dream about an opening scene where Jim comes out of a plastic-surgery operation. In the end, it was agreed they should just introduce a new actor and not really point it out, however, Cubby's dream proved useful in explaining a different-looking Blofeld (and his doubles).

Charles Gray's Blofeld was much lighter in style and tone – even appearing in drag at one point – which probably wouldn't have suited Telly Savalas. Again, Blofeld eludes capture, but, thanks to the ongoing legal battle with Kevin McClory, doesn't return to the series for a full ten years, and then isn't actually referred to as Blofeld: John Hollis supplied his body and Robert Rietty his voice in the pre-title sequence of *For Your Eyes Only*. I ended up dropping him down an industrial chimney. Did he survive? Who knows?

BELOW: In *Diamonds Are Forever*, having undergone plastic surgery, Blofeld has yet another face – this one looking suspiciously like Charles Gray.

ABOVE: Oddjob's custom-made steel-brimmed hat.

BELOW: Rosa Klebb's poison-tipped shoe and the design sketch by Pinewood effects engineer Bert Luxford.

SO MANY FOES

Aside from the esteemed Number 1, SPECTRE has offered up many foes to Jimbo. There was of course crazed genius Dr. Julius No, as played by Joseph Wiseman, and as with all great Bond villains he has a physical anomaly: in developing nuclear energy for no-good uses, he lost his hands and they were replaced by a metallic pair. The good doctor actually met his maker after being lowered into his own reactor coolant and, being unable to grip anything with his metal hands, it was good night Vienna.

When casting ideas for *Dr. No* were first mooted, Ian Fleming suggested his friend Noël Coward to play the villainous doctor. A telegram was sent to the Master, which he answered with, 'Dr. No? No! No! No!' Harry Saltzman is said to have then chosen Wiseman because of his performance in a dark 1951 movie called *Detective Story*.

Ken Adam's futuristic set of No's base – and Ken's sets are always a major contribution to the nutcase megalomaniac villain's thoughts of superiority – featured a huge aquarium in the background of the dining room. It was described as being constructed from convex glass to give the impression of a ten-times magnification, making 'minnows look like whales'. A classic touch was added on set when a reproduction of a Goya painting of the Duke of Wellington, which had actually been stolen in 1961, was placed on an easel next to the stairs; Bond stops to look as he passes it. Thankfully, the real portrait was recovered in 1965.

Rosa Klebb, as played by Lotte Lenya, was also known as 'Number 3' in SPECTRE ranking. A thoroughly unpleasant lady with a penchant for peculiar shoes, in *From Russia With Love* we learn that Klebb secretly defected from SMERSH and used her former rank to deceive and recruit Tatiana Romanova, who in turn assisted the British in acquiring a Russian Lektor decoding device. By sending in Red Grant (Robert Shaw) to kill Bond, the Lektor would then fall into the hands of SPECTRE, or so she reckoned.

Grant is first introduced to audiences in the pre-title sequence – the premiere in the series – stalking a 007 lookalike around SPECTRE Island. It was inspired by the film *L'année dernière à Marienbad*, which had a lush garden setting, complete with eerie statues to stalk amongst. Director Terence Young dressed the gardens at Pinewood Studios and introduced a few false hedgerows to achieve a similar setting.

When Red Grant later gave himself away as an imposter to Bond on board the Orient Express by not knowing his wine, one of the classic Bond fights ensued. Set in the confines of a train

carriage, although the fight took just a few minutes of screen time, it took weeks of rehearsal.

And then there was Auric Goldfinger as played by German actor Gert Fröbe. He wasn't a member of SPECTRE, though I'm sure they'd have welcomed him. His plan was simple, and known as Operation Grandslam: amass huge wealth through gold bullion, and then increase its value tenfold by setting off a nuclear device inside the US gold depository, Fort Knox, rendering it untouchable.

Auric Goldfinger was named after Ian Fleming's neighbour, Ernő Goldfinger, a rather eminent architect and furniture designer.

ABOVE: Goldfinger was the first villain to lend his name to a Bond film title. German-born Gert Fröbe played the titular character, and his Korean Man Friday (Oddjob) was played by Harold Sakata.

It was said that some of his less endearing character traits were borrowed from him too. When the book was published in 1959, Ernő Goldfinger was unhappy and consulted his lawyers, prompting Fleming to suggest renaming the character 'Goldprick', but Goldfinger eventually settled out of court in return for his legal costs, six copies of the novel and an agreement that the character's first name 'Auric' would always be used.

In both the novel and film, Goldfinger is aided in his crimes by his manservant, Oddjob, a mute, monstrously strong Korean who ruthlessly eliminates any threat to his employer's affairs. Another notable feature was Oddjob's rather unusual taste in headgear.

When Jim's captured by Goldfinger, we really do fear for his life. He's laid out, spread-eagled on a table, hands and feet secured, with a powerful laser rising between his legs.

Bond: 'Do you expect me to talk?'

Goldfinger: 'No, Mr Bond. I expect you to die.'

Ah, classic lines.

In fact, the laser beam was added optically later on and the cutting effect was achieved by F/X engineer Bert Luxford lying underneath the aforementioned table, on his back, with a blowtorch. He slowly cut up towards Sean's groin – having only a chalked line to tell him where he should stop. Sean was, understandably, rather anxious.

ABOVE AND BELOW:
Goldfinger's lethal laser, seen here on set and in the Pinewood workshop, was not really able to cut through metal. Its beam was added in to the film later, optically.

LIP SYNCH

Gert Fröbe was cast after he impressed the producers and director Guy Hamilton as paedophile killer Schrott in the German/Swiss version of *The Pledge*. They asked his agent if he spoke English, and the reply came back, 'Of course he does'. When Fröbe arrived at Pinewood to start shooting, he walked over to Guy Hamilton and said, 'How do you do? I am very pleased to be here.'

Guy asked if his hotel was OK. 'How do you do?' Gert replied. 'I am very pleased to be here.' It soon became evident their lead villain

spoke no English whatsoever!

Undaunted, Guy suggested they could dub him later, and asked Gert to speak the lines phonetically. In order to maintain a believable delivery pace, Guy asked him to speak very quickly rather than think about the words too much. In rushes the next day, the two producers couldn't believe what they were seeing and hearing. It was total babble. Guy told them not to worry, and drafted in Michael Collins to provide the English voice, and his delivery matched the lip movement of Gert Fröbe brilliantly well.

Emilio Largo was a force to be reckoned with as 'Number 2' in *Thunderball*. Italian actor Adolfo Celi played the villainous Largo, who used his talents well as head of extortion operations at SPECTRE. Fleming described Largo as a 'ruthless Neapolitan black marketeer and fence who moved to riskier and more profitable ventures on the international crime scene', and his black eye patch gave him a certain evil *je ne sais quoi*. Adolfo also had quite a strong accent and his voice was dubbed by Robert Reitty.

Blaxploitation movies were fast becoming popular in 1970s cinema, and screenwriter Tom Mankiewicz thought it would be very daring to use black villains in *Live And Let Die*, especially with the Black Panthers and other racial movements being very active. The 'swinging sixties' had romanticized the use of soft drugs, but in the early 1970s it was taken a step further by drug barons and counterculture. This all combined for an exciting plot in which Jimmy Bond tackled the drug barons head on, or at least Harlem drug lord Mr Big, whose plan was to distribute the world's largest cache of heroin, free of charge, on the open market. It would drive other drug cartels out of business, increase the number of addicts, and give Mr Big and his alter ego, poppy-farming Dr Kananga, a monopoly.

As director Guy Hamilton was a jazz fan, he suggested filming in New Orleans and decided to use an opulent New Orleans jazz funeral as the starting point in the film, and as a cover to enable the villainous Mr Big to make a few agents disappear. Then, while searching for Kananga's island retreat (in Jamaica), the crew

ABOVE: Emilio Largo (Adolfo Celi) was SPECTRE Number 2 in *Thunderball*. A nasty piece of work if ever there was one.

discovered a crocodile farm owned by a certain Dr. Kananga (after passing a sign warning that 'trespassers will be eaten'). The farm was incorporated into the script and that inspired Mankiewicz to name Mr Big's alter ego after the owner.

Yaphet Kotto was cast as Kananga/Mr Big, the first (and to date only) African American villain in a 007 adventure.

GOLDEN MOMENTS

For my second outing, my old pal – and Ian Fleming's cousin, as it happened – Christopher Lee was cast as my opponent, Francisco Scaramanga, aka *The Man With The Golden Gun*. Christopher and I had worked together on a film called *Trottie True* right back in 1949 when I was starting out, and then again in an episode of the TV series *Ivanhoe* in the 1950s.

On *The Man With The Golden Gun* I used to tease Christopher mercilessly about his role as Dracula and, just before the director

LEFT: Nick Nack (Hervé Villechaize) was the diminutive hired help of Scaramanga, and as this photo indicates, he was quite a ladies' man.

BELOW: In *The Man With The Golden Gun* I faced up to my old friend Christopher Lee.

RIGHT: A rather provocative poster image for the film, featuring Christopher Lee's hand.

BELOW: Remember the bullet with 007 on that arrived in M's office? Well, it was a custom-made, 4.2-millimetre, golden (23-carat gold with traces of nickel) dum-dum bullet.

called 'Action', I would lean over and say, 'Go on, Chris, make your eyes go red!'

Then there was the time we first entered the mouth of the cave on James Bond Island, which was replicated back at Pinewood as Scaramanga's HQ. A mass of bats flew out towards us. Without flinching, Christopher held up his hand and said, 'Not now, Stanislav!'

He looked sheepishly at me and said, 'You're going to use that against me, aren't you?'

Me? As if!

Scaramanga is assisted by the diminutive Nick Nack, as played by Hervé Villechaize. Dear Hervé was a fun character – and sex

mad! I asked him how many girls he'd had while we were shooting in Hong Kong.

'Forty-five,' he replied in his squeaky French voice.

'Ah!' I said. 'But it doesn't count if you paid them.'

'Even when I offer to pay sometimes they refuse me,' he added sadly.

He trotted up to Maud Adams in the lobby of the Peninsula Hotel in Hong Kong one morning, tugged on her knee-length skirt and looked up to say, 'Maud, tonight I am going to creep into your room, climb under the duvet and make mad passionate love to you.'

Unfazed, Maud replied, 'If I find out you have, I'll be very cross.'

Poor Hervé.

Karl Stromberg was very nearly a member of SPECTRE, as I mentioned earlier. However, his bizarre undersea ideology was enough to make him a stand-alone villain, especially with his quirky webbed fingers. Curt Jurgens played Stromberg, and we became great friends. He introduced me to Gstaad, and when I realized I'd have to find a home outside of the crippling UK tax regime, he offered my family and me his chalet in the Swiss resort to see if we'd like the town. We did, and moved there.

OPPOSITE: Karl Stromberg (as played by Curt Jurgens) in *The Spy Who Loved Me*, one of my more charismatic adversaries. Note the vice-like grip in which he holds both me and Barbara Bach-to-Front.

THE TALLER THEY COME ...

Every good villain has a good henchman, of course. The most memorable of all has to be Jaws, as played by my good friend Richard Kiel.

Richard, who stands seven foot two and a half inches tall, was cast after script supervisor June 'Randy' Randall saw him in an episode of the US TV series *Barbary Coast*. She knew the team was looking for a very tall actor – and they didn't come much taller than Richard.

When we filmed the scenes among the ruined Karnak temples in Egypt, Lewis Gilbert told Richard that for one shot he needed to be up in the scaffolding, high above Jimmy Bond. Richard went pale, and said he suffered with vertigo. 'Hey, I don't even like being this tall!' he exclaimed.

Faced with what seemed an insurmountable problem, my stunt double, Martin Grace, said he'd impersonate Richard, and used

ABOVE: Richard Kiel as Jaws was voted the best Bond villain in a recent poll.

BELOW: His teeth could munch through solid cables – if he'd had his Weetabix.

pieces of orange peel wrapped in tin foil for Jaws' 'metal' teeth. As it turned out, Martin mimicked Richard's every move so well that when Richard's mother saw it she asked him how on earth – with his fear of heights – he managed to film that sequence. She wouldn't believe it wasn't him.

Of course, Jaws got his name from the ominous, glinting steel teeth he wore. Poor devil, they were so uncomfortable to wear – Richard could only keep them in for about half a minute at a time. The comical expressions he had to convey were quite the opposite of what he was feeling, with an overwhelming urge to gag!

Jaws' popularity stemmed from the humour Richard injected into the character, and we all agreed he made a superb villain. In the script, he died at the end of *The Spy Who Loved Me*; however, Cubby felt it could be worth saving him, and the scene was re-written. Jaws didn't drown, but popped up in the ocean and started swimming. That raised a round of applause at the premiere – especially from the youngsters.

He did of course return, in *Moonraker*, as did Hervé Villechaize … for a set visit. Our unit publicist thought he'd spotted a photo opportunity and asked if they'd pose together, as 'little and large' villains. Richard quite rightly said, 'I don't do freak photos.'

BELOW: Arriving on the *Moonraker* publicity trail – me and my two mates, Michael Lonsdale and Richard Kiel.

TO SPACE AND BEYOND!

Moonraker was filmed in Paris as an Anglo-French co-production under the 1965–79 film treaty. France had much more favourable taxation laws for the creative industries, and that was a great lure to Cubby in setting up the film there, but part of their qualifying criteria was that the lead villain had to be French. Hugo Drax was going to be played by James Mason, who coincidentally I worked with later that year in *North Sea Hijack*; I admired him greatly and thought it terrific casting. However, because of the qualifying criteria, bilingual Frenchman Michael Lonsdale was accordingly offered the part, and made a wonderfully underplayed yet menacing Drax. He became the first Bond villain to take a giant step for mankind, and perished in space.

Of course, once you've been to space, there isn't a lot further you can go with a Bond villain, and so it was decided to bring the next film, *For Your Eyes Only*, and its protagonists back to earth. The only problem, for Jim, is that he couldn't really be sure who the bad guy was: Kristatos (Julian Glover) or Columbo (Topol)?

It really is a much more grounded story, with the villains being the good old, dependable Russians – keen to get their hands on the British ATAC device. The Soviets were at it again in *Octopussy*, too. Crazed General Orlov (Steven Berkoff) thought he could make the West

disarm by setting off a nuclear device inside an American airbase in West Germany. He and Kamal Khan (Louis Jourdan) used the Octopussy Circus as a front for their dastardly plans.

By the time of my swansong, *A View To A Kill*, technology was becoming the world's major boom industry, and accordingly became the subject for our original screenplay. Our villain, Max Zorin, played by Christopher Walken, was the product of nasty Nazi medical experimentation during World War II, in which pregnant women were injected with massive quantities of steroids in an attempt to create 'super-children'. Most of the pregnancies failed, but the few that did survive went on to become extraordinarily intelligent individuals – but with a taste for world domination and more than a streak of ruthlessness.

My only sadness with this film was the sheer amount of violence, gunfire and explosions, killing scores of innocent Zorin employees in the finale. It seemed a little over the top in my mind, and not quite in the Bond tradition.

With détente and a warming Cold War, the Russians obviously couldn't be Bond's enemy for much longer, but in *The Living Daylights* General Koskov, played by Dutch actor Jeroen Krabbé, played on the thawing relations to draw Britain into a double-crossing plot, which would help him eliminate the head of the KGB and leave the way clear to take over.

A complete change of tone was ushered in with Franz Sanchez in *Licence To Kill*: he ran a drug cartel from South America to Asia. Played by Robert Davi, Sanchez had an interesting choice of pet in a large green iguana that wore a rather fetching diamond collar. I found the iguana quite diverting, but the story was one of personal revenge for the murder of Felix Leiter's new wife, Della, and, for me, it became far too dark in style and content.

It was interesting, therefore, to see that the next Bond villain – in *GoldenEye* in 1995 – was intent on taking over control of the aforenamed satellite and using it for personal profit – back to the good old baddies! Formerly known as 'Agent 006', Alex Trevelyan, played by Sean Bean, was a contemporary of Jim's from MI6. Apparently, Sean Bean had been considered for the role of Jimbo at one point, but became a baddie instead. That's what happens, you see.

TOP TO BOTTOM: Louis Jourdan was Kamal Khan in *Octopussy*.

Christopher Walken as Max Zorin in *A View To A Kill*.

Sean Bean played Alec Trevelyan in *GoldenEye*.

Robert Davi played drug baron Franz Sanchez in *Licence To Kill*.

Of course, many Bond villains are modelled on real people, or should I say real circumstances in which they could exist.

❦ Take Elliott Carver (Jonathan Pryce, above right) in *Tomorrow Never Dies*: a global media magnate who wanted to expand his empire by any means, and in particular into China. Who does that remind you of?

❦ Oil is a massive player in the world energy stakes. Control the pipelines, you control the wealth. Elektra King (Sophie Marceau, right) thought it acceptable to destroy Istanbul and thus control the Bosphorus oil supplies in *The World Is Not Enough*. That's not nice.

❦ Satellites orbit our earth, and control all manner of things. Control one of them with a powerful death ray attached, and the world would be in trouble – as Gustav Graves (Toby Stephens, right) realized in *Die Another Day*.

❦ But who finances the crooks and their schemes? One such person is LeChiffre, the terrorists' banker. Only thing is, he needed to turn a profit on investments left in his care, and made unwise decisions. He had to win it back in a high-stakes poker game to prevent the mysterious head of Quantum, Mr White (Jesper Christensen, right), from becoming upset in *Casino Royale*.

❦ Mr White and Quantum are also behind Dominic Greene's (Mathieu Amalric, right) attempts to control water in Bolivia – or at least I think that was the plot – in *Quantum Of Solace*. Mr Greene didn't survive, but Mr White is still out there. I just hope I don't bump into him!

BOND
ON
GIRLS

JAMES BOND 007
CONTRE "Dr. NO"
(Dr. NO)

BOND ON GIRLS

PREVIOUS PAGES: The most iconic of all Bond girl poses – Shirley Eaton was painted gold, head to toe, as the tragic Jill Masterson.

LEFT: Ursula Andress was voted 'Best Bond Girl of All Time' by readers of one national newspaper in 2008. She also received a Golden Globe as 'New Star of the Year' for her role in *Dr. No*.

How does one describe a 'Bond girl'? Bond girls are considered to be 'ubiquitous symbols of glamour and sophistication', according to Robert A. Caplen in his book *Shaken & Stirred: The Feminism of James Bond*, that is. Bond girls are certainly bewitching, beguiling and memorable but they are not always necessarily *just* the victims of Bond's charm: many villainesses, allies and co-workers are given the moniker too, as is my wife Kristina – my favourite Bond girl of all.

In Fleming's books, Bond girls always seemed to be in their mid-twenties, a decade or so younger than Jim, though in *Goldfinger* Fleming wrote that Bond suspected Pussy Galore was in her early thirties. An older woman? Perish that thought!

BELOW: Eunice Gayson was the very first Bond girl. Her famous red dress was in fact a last-minute change, and as it wasn't made to measure, she had to use a few strategically placed clothes pegs to hold it together!

BEAUTY IS IN THE EYE ...

Needless to say, all Bond girls are very beautiful, more often than not sporting a light sun tan, and with their eyes and mouths widely spaced – or so wrote Ian Fleming. Their eyes, by the way, are usually blue, but in *Diamonds Are Forever* Tiffany Case's are chatoyant – 'varying with the light from grey to grey-blue' – while in *Goldfinger* Pussy Galore has deep-violet eyes, the only truly violet eyes Bond had ever seen.

Yes, they all usually have exotic-sounding names too. In addition to the aforementioned, we have Suki, Vesper, Honey, Tatiana, Solitaire, Chew Me, Bibi, Octopussy, Mayday, Kara, Lupe, Paris and Elektra. Suggestive, sexy and very, very Bondian.

Fleming indicated that most of the Bond girls were sexually experienced by the time they met 007, which is probably just as well. However, not all of their experiences had been positive, with histories of sexual violence often a contributory factor in alienating them from men – until Jim arrived on the scene. Jim, meanwhile, I should add, lost his virginity on his first visit to Paris when he was sweet sixteen.

Though this darker backcloth to the characters is largely absent from the films, many Bond girls do face some abuse on screen – Domino (Claudine Auger) at the hands of Largo's cigarette and ice in *Thunderball*; Andrea Anders (Maud Adams) in *The Man With The Golden Gun* is hurt by the dastardly Francisco Scaramanga; Lupe Lamora (Talisa Soto) in *Licence To Kill* is whipped by Franz Sanchez … perhaps these events were behind their determination to resist Bond at first?

But Jimmy's charms win through … even in the case of lesbian Pussy Galore when, in bed, Bond says, 'They told me you only liked women,' and she tellingly replies it was because 'I never met a man before.'

You have to laugh. To think Bond could turn a gay woman is quite comical. But then again, Judi Dench's M did describe Jim as being 'a sexist, misogynist dinosaur. A relic of the Cold War…' in *GoldenEye*, so he'd probably like to think he could.

BELOW: Margaret Nolan played Dink in *Goldfinger*. A well-rounded role!

Cubby Broccoli admitted that Honor Blackman had been cast on the back of her success in *The Avengers*, despite the fact that the American audience had never even seen the programme. He said, 'The Brits would love her because they knew her as Mrs Gale, the Yanks would like her because she was so good, it was a perfect combination.'

One time I was doing an interview with Jimmy Tarbuck on *Sunday Night at the London Palladium* and Tarbuck said:

'You're the Saint, Sean Connery is Bond, Patrick McGoohan is Danger Man and Patrick MacNee is in *The Avengers* ... do you ever meet up?'

I said, 'Yeah, sure.'

'Do you go out together?'

'Yeah,' I said.

'Pussy Galore?'

'Well, we don't go looking for it ...' I replied.

I'm still not sure how we got away with it!

BEWARE NUMBER ONE

Bond rarely limits himself to just one conquest per film. The pattern established by Cubby and Harry – and still honoured to this day – usually sees anyone sleeping with Bond in the first reel bumped off before the end of the second. So beware young actresses.

Roald Dahl summed it up best when he spoke about being contracted to write the screenplay for *You Only Live Twice* (1967): '"You put in three girls," the producers said, "girl number one is pro-Bond. She stays around roughly for the first reel of the picture, then she is bumped off by the enemy, preferably in Bond's arms.

'"Girl number two is anti-Bond and usually captures him, and he has to save himself by knocking her out with his sexual charm and power. She gets killed in an original (usually grisly) fashion mid-way through the film. The third girl will manage to survive to the end of the film."'

To date, only two Bond girls have actually turned the formula around and captured Bond's heart – though neither lived very long, proving you can't tamper with the recipe too much. In *On Her Majesty's Secret Service*, Tracy di Vicenzo (Diana Rigg) married Bond, though she was shot dead soon after the ceremony by Irma Bunt and Ernst Stavro Blofeld. The second to wed was Vesper Lynd (Eva Green) in *Casino Royale*. Bond professes his love for her and resigns from MI6 in order that they can have a normal life together. Later, he learns she was actually a double agent working for his enemies at Quantum (in the film) – the enemy organization ostensibly kidnapped her former lover and was blackmailing her to secure her cooperation. She died by drowning in a lift in a building under renovation. Realizing his betrayal and loss in equal measure, Bond confirmed, 'The bitch is dead' – one of the most intense lines of all Fleming's novels, which was also used in the film.

FAQS

Among the most frequently asked questions I am asked in interviews (and I assume this is true of any other retired 007) is, 'Who is your favourite Bond girl?'

'Oh! How original!' I exclaim. 'No one has ever asked me that before.'

I never give an answer as I think it is terribly unfair to name one co-star as being any better than another; you immediately upset someone. 'What was wrong with me?' they cry out.

Avoiding naming names also allows me to talk about some leading ladies without actually identifying them, though if I drop the odd hint, you might put two and two together.

In the 1960s, while playing Simon Templar, I was being interviewed by a television station and the journalist started off with, 'You've played Ivanhoe, Maverick and now the Saint … you must have got through a lot of leading ladies in your time.'

'You can't say that!' I cried.

My interrogator didn't seem to realize what he was saying. He re-phrased it and said virtually the same thing again. I cringe whenever I see the clip.

Normally when you have a scene involving kissing a lady (or I guess a man if you fancy it), you never actually go in for the kiss during rehearsal as it tends to smudge make-up and ruffle hair. You just go through the motions, move in close, say 'and they kiss' and get on with the rest of the scene. In *The Spy Who Loved Me* I rehearsed one such scene with an Italian actress, and it all seemed to go rather well. Lewis Gilbert leaned over and said, 'Can we have a sample of the kiss, dear?'

Suddenly from across the stage floor, this long snake-like tongue shot at me at the speed of light, worked its way around my teeth like dental floss and plunged deep into my throat. I was quite taken aback.

There is certainly no romance in a love scene, save that for the dressing room, if you're lucky – and if your wife ever walks in on you, heed the advice of Burt

LEFT TOP: Sean and Martine Beswicke in *Thunderball*. Martine also appeared in the gypsy fight sequence in *From Russia With Love*.

LEFT BELOW: Mollie Peters played Patricia in *Thunderball*, and helped soothe Jim's stress.

BELOW: The happiest days of Bond's life. Mr and Mrs James Bond in *On Her Majesty's Secret Service*.

Lancaster as relayed to me by Tony Curtis: 'Just continue, and when you get home, explain they have people that look like you on the film.'

Far from being a romantic moment of intimacy shared by two people, a film love scene is often witnessed by fifty or sixty crew members, many being hairy-arsed technicians in the rafters clenching fists and shouting, 'Go on, Rog! Give her one for us!' It does rather put one off one's stride. And if there's mention on the call sheet of a love scene, or one of at least partial nudity, it always amazes me how the crew size swells and we tend to inherit workers from adjacent stages and productions.

ABOVE: My good friend Jill St John, Mrs Robert Wagner these days, showing that diamonds are a girl's best friend in 1971.

RIGHT: My first leading lady, Jane Seymour. In the casting session, she removed her hat, shook her head, and let her long hair fall out. There was no question of anyone else after that.

WHO WILL IT BE?

There is always a huge interest in who is going to be cast as the next Bond girl, not least among the crew, and inevitably there is a press conference to introduce her. She then has a few minutes to talk about being 'different from the normal Bond girls' by 'being independent, tough, intelligent and a new type of girl'. They all say it.

Many girls, particularly in the early films, were cast because of their ravishing good looks. There's nothing wrong with that, and I'm no sexist either, let me add. If they happened to have rather large busts, that certainly sealed their involvement as far as Cubby was concerned. He was what you'd call 'a boob man'. Though he also once remarked, on set, while looking at one of the lovely beauties wandering about, that she had a 'particularly lovely derrière'. The lady seemingly also had particularly good hearing, as she turned, pounced and told Cubby he was a 'sexist, misogynist swine' and went into a long diatribe about how women have been kept down over the centuries by men like him, and how women are actually better than men, and how dare he treat her like a bimbo.

Another time we incurred the wrath of one of our leading ladies was when Lewis Gilbert offered me a little direction: 'Roger, when you come in and she sees you ...'

'She! *She*?' exclaimed the intelligent, tough, independent beauty. 'I have a name and it is ******!' and she spelled it out in a very loud voice.

'I wasn't talking to you, dear, I was talking to *him*,' Lewis replied rather nonchalantly.

On another occasion, when giving direction to the same lady, Lewis suggested, 'You come in here, and follow him over there.'

'Why do I always have to follow *him*?' she asked.

'Because, dear, he is f***ing James Bond!' Lewis helpfully replied.

To be perfectly honest, ladies cast in a Bond film were

ABOVE: His and Hers outfits came as standard on this set. Lois Chiles as Dr Holly Goodhead. In explaining away her character's name to her father she said, 'I'm a doctor, with a very good head on my shoulders.' Well, what else would it mean?

primarily signed because of their beauty, charm, charisma and, oh yes, a little acting ability helped too. It's no great secret that Nikki Van Der Zyl dubbed many of the voices in the sixties films, because their accents were considered a little too heavy, but their outstanding beauty made them much sought-after individuals.

Not all were very experienced in screen acting technique, and I recall all too well a sequence when cigarette smoke (or actually a stun gas) had to be blown into my face. For smoke, talcum powder was substituted, and instead of blowing it slightly to the side of my face the lady in question blew it straight into my eye – not just in one take, but in four. It wasn't one of my favourite days.

Just ahead of a rather large set piece, involving big explosions, another leading lady wondered why my make-up man had presented me with a set of earplugs.

I explained the noise would be rather deafening. 'Oh well, that won't bother me as I'll stand near you.' I had to explain that it was *me* they were trying to kill.

Towards the end of my tenure, I believe I was extraordinarily patient and good-willed with two leading ladies who became obsessive about dashing back to their handbags after every take to re-apply lipstick and face powder. I'd wait and wait for them to reappear with another layer, say a line and then disappear again. This went on incessantly and wasted so much time. When they weren't looking, I decided to take the lipsticks out of the bags, and built a little pile of them, along with powder puffs and mirrors, but the ladies never really noticed as, without flinching, they dipped their hand in to their bottomless bags to produce yet another one. Heaven only knows how many sets they owned.

The character of Goodnight appears in Ian Fleming's books *On Her Majesty's Secret Service* and *You Only Live Twice* as Bond's secretary, before becoming a fully-fledged Bond girl in *The Man With The Golden Gun*. Britt Ekland was a great fan of the books and lobbied the producers to cast her in the role. Then, as is often the way in this business, she read an article saying Swedish actress Maud Adams had been confirmed as the next Bond girl. Her heart sank. Of course, she then received a call to say she had got the part after all, Maud was playing the villain's girlfriend, Andrea Anders.

On James Bond Island the crew rigged up explosions for the finale of the movie, when Scaramanga's HQ goes up in smoke. Everything was carefully timed for us to run from A to B as the explosions went off. Rather worryingly, the cameras were set up offshore on boats.

Guy Hamilton called 'Action!' and I ran. But Britt hesitated for a moment. I was faced with a split-second decision: carry on running, or be the gallant hero and go back for her. I turned around, grabbed and pulled her forward, towards me. I then felt all the tiny hairs on her back singe after the first explosion. I'm such a hero.

Barbara Bach, former model and

LEFT: The lovely Cassandra Harris played Countess Lisl. She was joined by her young husband for the premiere. Cubby thought he could be a candidate for Bond ...

BOTTOM LEFT: If you're going to fool around in a wardrobe, I suggest you do it with the delectable Madeline Smith.

BELOW: My Swedish friend Britt Ekland. *Bon appétit*, and Goodnight.

wife-to-be of Ringo Starr, was quite a different Bond girl in that she was the Soviet oppo of Jim. As agent Triple-X she perhaps had the most prominent starring role since Diana Rigg in *On Her Majesty's Secret Service*.

Cubby was under huge pressure to get everything right on this film, and I know he had spent a long time looking for the perfect girl. He answered the question of why Barbara Bach with his usual aplomb: 'There isn't an actress today, with the possible exception of Barbra Streisand, who can open a film. We explored a certain lady in Hollywood who commands a $500,000 fee and that blew her right out of the box for me because she'd contribute no more than Barbara Bach.'

I used to pull her leg, of course, dubbing her Barbara-Back-to-Front, and in Luxor when we left for the location each morning we'd always pass hundreds of black-burka-clad women.

'The nuns are out early again,' I said, rather lightheartedly.

'Oh, are they all Catholics here?' she asked earnestly.

She and Ringo are now neighbours of mine in Monaco, and we still see each other from time to time.

A ONE-WOMAN BOND

In my final outing, I was joined by Mary Stavin, Fiona Fullerton, Tanya Roberts and Grace Jones.

A day in a hot tub with Fiona could never be considered 'work' really, could it? And floating away on board a submarine with Mary Stavin must be many men's dream. As to the others, I'll leave it there, I think.

Post-me, in the mid-1980s, HIV/AIDS was becoming a major issue in the world and Bond writers felt that Timothy Dalton's new 007 should not be as promiscuous as my 007. He therefore became a one-woman Bond with Maryam d'Abo's Kara Milovy

LEFT: Another obligatory posse. Do I complain?

FAR LEFT: Maud Adams as *Octopussy*.

BELOW FAR LEFT: She who shall remain nameless.

BELOW LEFT: 'Would you like it harder, Miss Fullerton?' – the massage I meant! A de-briefing scene from *A View To A Kill*.

BELOW RIGHT: In *Quantum Of Solace* Olga Kurylenko provided Bond's back-up girl, Camille.

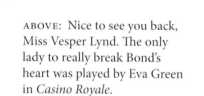

ABOVE: Nice to see you back, Miss Vesper Lynd. The only lady to really break Bond's heart was played by Eva Green in *Casino Royale*.

ABOVE RIGHT: Whereas Paris Carver, an old flame, sadly went to bed with Bond too soon after the film started. I keep telling them not to bed him in the first reel or they'll die, but they don't listen.

RIGHT: Famke Janssen and Isabella Scorupco were the two female leads in *GoldenEye*.

in *The Living Daylights* but stepped up a gear in *Licence To Kill* with two romantic interests, Carey Lowell and Talisa Soto.

When Pierce came along, the team took the decision to introduce a few more well-known actresses to the franchise, such as Teri Hatcher, Michelle Yeoh, Denise Richards and Halle Berry – who won her Oscar mid-production on *Die Another Day* for the movie *Monster's Ball*. In a nod to *Dr. No*, Halle emerged from the ocean in a sexy bikini in the film's only main location; the majority of filming was studio-bound. She proved such a popular character that producers felt a *Jinx* spin-off movie would be a sure-fire hit. Neil Purvis and Robert Wade were engaged to write a script; Stephen Frears was reportedly keen to direct and all looked set ... until MGM got nervous about the budget, and felt they'd rather have another Bond film than risk launching a new franchise. MGM cited 'creative differences'.

With Daniel Craig came Eva Green as Vesper Lynd. The character's name, incidentally, is a pun on West Berlin, signifying Vesper's divided loyalties as a double agent under Soviet control. Eva became the fifth French actress to be cast as a Bond girl. Following in her footsteps was Ukrainian-born Olga Kurylenko in *Quantum Of Solace* as Camille, with a backstory of child abuse akin to Ian Fleming's original flawed heroines.

BELOW: A more feisty Bond girl came in the shape of Pam Bouvier in *Licence To Kill,* played by Carey Lowell.

FAR RIGHT: The twentieth Bond film, in the fortieth year, paid homage to some of the earlier films, most notable here with Halle Berry re-creating Ursula Andress's famous scene in *Dr. No*.

RIGHT: Maryam d'Abo was the only Bond girl in *The Living Daylights*, when worries about HIV/AIDS were at their height.

BELOW: Christmas Jones was played by Denise Williams, and in her case proved Christmas came more than once a year.

Moneypenny

The lovely Lois Maxwell was a Canadian actress whom I first met way back during my time at RADA. We often appeared in the same student plays.

In 1962 Lois contacted her old friend director Terence Young and asked if there might be a part for her in his next film, as her husband had recently suffered a heart attack and they desperately needed the income. Terence said there were two possible parts: Sylvia Trench, Bond's love interest; or Miss Moneypenny. Lois read the script and didn't much care for the Sylvia Trench role, as it featured a scantily dressed scene with 007, so she opted for Moneypenny and received £200 for two days' work.

Alongside her role in the Bond movies, Lois appeared with me in an episode of *The Saint* and *The Persuaders!* before we resumed our on-stage association when I took on the role of Jimmy Bond.

It's interesting to note that despite her worldwide fame, Lois's total screen time as Moneypenny in her fourteen films was less than twenty minutes, and she spoke fewer

LEFT: The one and only Lois Maxwell in the role she loved.
ABOVE: Samantha Bond (no relation) played Moneypenny in all the Pierce Brosnan films.
ABOVE RIGHT: Pamela Salem was Sean Connery's choice for the role in *Never Say Never Again*.
ABOVE, FAR RIGHT: Caroline Bliss was a two-time Moneypenny for a two-time Bond, Timothy Dalton. She had a penchant for Barry Manilow records!
RIGHT: Two of a kind, Lois with Desmond Llewelyn – how I miss them both.

than 200 words. That's the power of Bond for you.

It was a huge shock to hear of Lois's death in 2007. She was always fun, wonderful company to be in and was absolutely perfect casting. Towards the end of my tenure as Jimbo, Lois said to Cubby that she would like to see Moneypenny become the new M. Cubby smiled and said, 'I don't think we can have a female head of the Secret Service.'

It was a great pity that after I moved out of Bond they didn't take her on to continue in the Timothy Dalton films, but I guess a younger Bond flirting with an older Moneypenny wasn't to be.

Other Miss Moneypennys include Caroline Bliss, Samantha Bond and – in the unofficial *Never Say Never Again* – Pamela Salem. Call me old-fashioned if you will, but there'll only ever be one Miss Moneypenny for me.

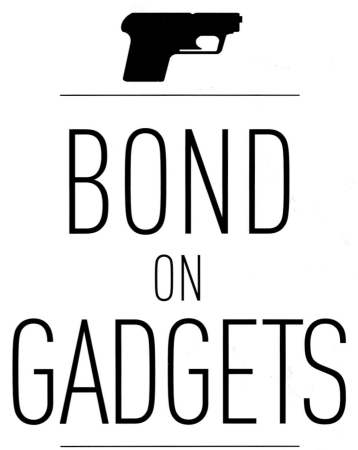

BOND
ON
GADGETS

BOND ON GADGETS

Almost every Bond film features a trip into Q-Branch, an underground Aladdin's cave-like bunker beneath the power desks of MI6, where a group of boffins led by their Quartermaster feverishly develop and invent wonderful gadgets, gizmos and accoutrements for the field operatives of Her Majesty's Secret Service. It's unclear just how many of these devices are ever returned; certainly if Jim is a yardstick then very few come back intact.

FINDING Q

While being one of the most well known and favourite of the returning characters, Q's origins are not terribly clear. There is a reference to Q in Chapter 3 of Fleming's *Casino Royale*. M says to Bond, 'Go over a few days before the big game starts and get your hand in. Have a talk to Q about rooms and trains, and any equipment you want.'

Q-Branch features occasionally in the novels, supplying Bond with equipment and gadgets, but it is said by scholars that the true origin of the Q character lies in the first film, *Dr. No*. The secret service armourer, Major Boothroyd, replaces Jim's Beretta with a new Walther PPK. There is no direct reference to Boothroyd being associated with Q Branch, though the character was based on a real person who advised Fleming on changing Bond's weapon, Major Geoffrey Boothroyd.

In the next film, Desmond Llewelyn's character is referred to as the 'Equipments Officer', when he supplies Jim with his new attaché case, although he is credited as Boothroyd in the closing titles. Of course, forever after we knew him as Q, which to my mind is far less confusing.

PREVIOUS PAGES: We must get them in the shops for Christmas, Q.

LEFT: One of my first 007 gadgets. A radio transmitter housed in a hairbrush.

BELOW: The famous Walther PPK as presented to Jim by 'The Armourer' in *Dr. No*. The PPK was used in most of the films up to *Tomorrow Never Dies*, and then made a welcome return in *Quantum Of Solace*.

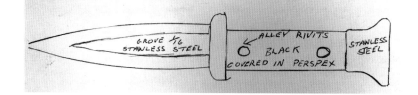

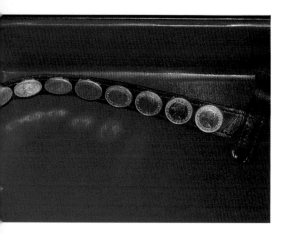

ABOVE: The first real gadget was the attaché case in *From Russia With Love*. It included twenty gold sovereigns, a throwing knife (this original design is by Pinewood effects engineer Bert Luxford), a tear gas canister and hidden ammunition.

RIGHT: The miniature spy camera from *On Her Majesty's Secret Service*, that Jim used to photograph Blofeld's Angels of Death.

Desmond Llewelyn played Q from 1963 to 1999 in a total of seventeen films. On screen, he was the gadget master who invented wonderful, never-before-seen devices, whereas off screen Desmond was a complete technophobe who struggled even to operate his own video recorder.

Desmond was not in *Dr. No*; that was Peter Burton. However, when Burton proved unavailable for *From Russia With Love*, Terence Young cast Desmond after remembering him from a few years earlier in a film called *They Were Not Divided*.

When Desmond arrived on set Terence asked him how he was going to play the character. 'As an English civil servant,' Desmond replied.

'No, you're a Welshman. Play it as a Welshman,' said Terence.

Desmond argued that a Welsh accent wouldn't carry the air of authority he felt the character should have. Nevertheless, he did as his director asked and put on a very broad Welsh accent.

'Well, look-see, I have this smashing case for you ... press this 'ere button and out pops a lovely knife ...'

'No, you're quite right,' said Terence. 'Play it as you thought.'

On the next film, *Goldfinger*, the character was really rounded out. Guy Hamilton told me that when Sean entered Q-Branch, Desmond stood up to greet him.

'No! No! No!' said Guy. 'You hate this man. He destroys everything you ever give him. You have nothing but contempt for him! Don't stand up to greet him.'

From then on, Q treated Bond with a circumspect irritation and established that wonderful love–hate relationship that lasted throughout the series.

Q's appearance in a Bond film was always highly anticipated, so you can imagine my disappointment when he wasn't in *Live And Let Die*. Apparently, it was decided that Bond was relying a little too much on gadgets, and Q would therefore be dropped.

However, there was such an outcry after the film's release that Q was immediately written back into the next film.

ABOVE AND LEFT: In Japan, Tiger Tanaka demonstrated the rocket-firing cigarette to Bond. They say smoking kills ...

LEFT: In *Goldfinger*, early GPS-style technology was employed in these two tracking devices. One was affixed to Auric Goldfinger's car while the other, smaller, device was hidden in Jim's shoe.

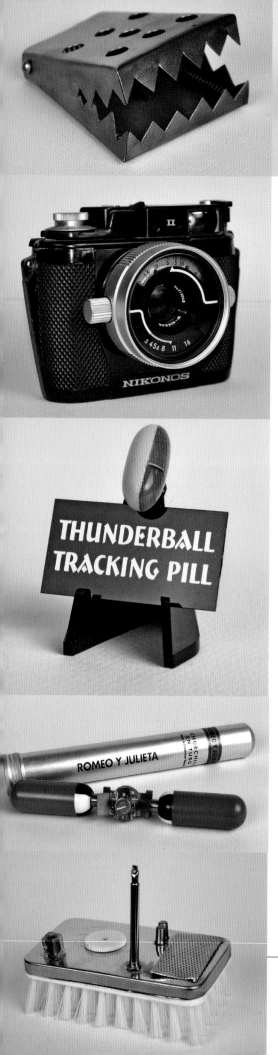

EVIL PERSONIFIED (ME, THAT IS)

Desmond always struggled to learn his dialogue, as after all, it was usually quite technical. I, being a caring and kind performer, noticed this early on in our working relationship and decided to take full, evil advantage of it.

Lewis Gilbert, who had directed *You Only Live Twice*, told me how Desmond complained about having to wear shorts in the movie. He didn't particularly like exposing his legs to the elements, and so whenever Desmond was in earshot I'd say quietly to Lewis, 'Oh, do you think it would work better if Q were to wear shorts in this sequence?'

'Eh? What?' said a worried Desmond.

'Yes, good idea, Rog!' Lewis replied. 'And perhaps in the next sequence too?'

Then I was particularly evil in rewriting his dialogue with the script supervisor, June Randall, and handing it to director John Glen to give to Desmond when he arrived at the studio. My rewrite was, of course, the biggest load of gibberish you can imagine. Desmond had already struggled to learn his lines and went into a blind panic when he was handed new pages so soon before being called on set. Of course, when he was called and saw me slowly shaking with stifled laughter, the penny dropped, as did a few choice words.

Sometimes we had 'idiot boards' on set, with his technical dialogue written in large text. As he glanced up to remind himself of the next line, the cards were peeled back one after the other. I helpfully rewrote some of those too. I like being helpful.

Desmond was always keen that his part be extended, and it finally was in *Licence To Kill* in 1989, but in an early draft of *The Man With The Golden Gun* by Tom Mankiewicz, he very nearly has an extra scene with me as Bond at Hong Kong airport. In the draft, Q tried to persuade 007 to take a gadget-laden camera with him on his trip. It featured gas ejection, which, by selecting various shutter speeds, instantly solidified anything in its path. Bond said something like, 'Most ingenious, but I'm sure there's one thing this contraption can't do ... take a photo.' Q castigated him for being facetious before adding, 'Yes you're right, but I'm working on it ...'

It was quite comical. Perhaps too comical? It was cut. After all, Q is quick to remind us, 'I never joke about my work, 007'.

A TASTE OF THINGS TO COME

While many of Q's gadgets – highly charged magnetic watches, remote-control cars, a signature gun, underwater cameras, wrist-triggered dart guns, GPS tracking devices, fake fingerprints and acid pens – seemed outlandish and improbable, Desmond always maintained that they were 'prototypes' and forerunners of things that did eventually make it into commercial production. In fact, so sought-after were some, that the highest powers in the land weren't averse to phoning through to the Bond production office for insights into their design. In 1965 the Royal Corps of Engineers, having seen *Thunderball*, asked the then art department draftsman Peter Lamont, 'How long can a man use your underwater breather device for?'

His answer was, 'How long can you hold your breath?'

Although more often than not exasperated, Q has always shown a warm and fatherly concern for 007's welfare, such as at Bond's wedding in *On Her Majesty's Secret Service*, when he pulled Jim to one side, to say that if there was ever anything Jim needed … oh and the occasion, at the behest of Miss Moneypenny, when Q secretly sneaked gadgets out of MI6 to help Bond survive his vendetta against the drug tyrant Sanchez in *Licence To Kill*. When he arrived, posing as Bond's uncle, he flatly told a dismissive 007, 'If it hadn't been for Q-Branch, you'd have been dead long ago.'

How true.

In 1999, aged eighty-five, Desmond voiced his concern that he may not be around for many more films. He asked the writers to pave the way for a new Q. In what was to be his last movie, *The World Is Not Enough*, Desmond's Q talks of his plan to retire and go fishing. A crestfallen Bond says, 'You're not planning on retiring any time soon, are you?'

FAR LEFT AND LEFT: Beware of pickpockets ... or should that be, beware pickpocketers. A finger trap slipped in the inside jacket pocket gives any hoodlum in search of your gun a nasty snap.

MIDDLE LEFT: The bug detector, used by Bond in his Istanbul hotel room. Walls have ears, you know.

LEFT: The Nikon underwater camera – a prototype for future technology, as were many of the early Q-Branch gadgets – was first seen in *Thunderball*.

LEFT: In *Thunderball*, Jim was issued with another tracking device, but this one used (harmless) radioactivity principles and took the form of an everyday pill.

LEFT: The underwater breather, which as well as appearing in *Thunderball*, made a return in *Die Another Day*. The air supply lasts for as long as you can hold your breath!

LEFT: The radio transmitter hairbrush was very neat.

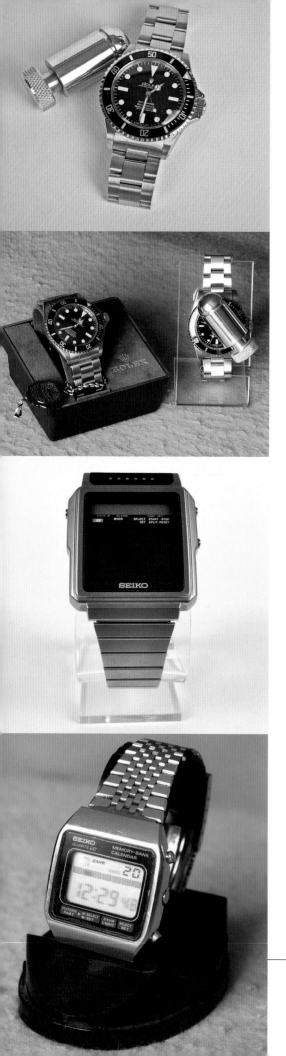

Q: 'I've always tried to teach you two things: First, never let them see you bleed.'

Bond: 'And the second?'

Q: 'Always have an escape plan.'

He is then lowered out of view.

When in 1998 Desmond asked me to pen a Foreword for his autobiography, simply entitled, *Q*, I wrote one of the things I missed most after leaving Bond was him. That was absolutely true. He bore my childish pranks so patiently and, being gadget mad (as my wife will attest), I used to love playing with all the gizmos in Q-Branch.

I was watching Sky news on Sunday 19 December 1999, when I heard the awful news that Desmond had been involved in a car accident. He was returning home to Bexhill from a book signing. He died from his injuries. I was devastated.

A few months later, I attended his memorial service in London and spoke of the gentle gentleman who, despite having hands the size of spades and a total incomprehension of what he was talking about, always managed to explain and demonstrate his devices with great skill and endear himself to millions of fans across the world.

With the reboot of the Bond series in 2006's *Casino Royale* and its successor, *Quantum Of Solace*, the character of Q did not appear, though gadgets were still very much in evidence.

Other actors to have played Q on film include John Cleese in

Die Another Day, Geoffrey Bayldon in 1967's *Casino Royale* and Alec McCowen in *Never Say Never Again*, with that wonderful line on Jim's return to Q-Branch, 'Good to see you, Mr Bond. Things have been awfully dull around here without you. I hope we're going to see some gratuitous sex and violence …'

GUNS 'N' AMMO

Think of 007 and you conjure up images of girls, gadgets and … guns. Yes, Jim's firearms have played as important a part of his adventures as anything else, and though he has carried many, in the films at least, there has always been one constant in his chamois leather holster – the Walther PPK.

However, the Beretta was the gun Fleming's literary Bond carried. It was described, by firearm enthusiast Geoffrey Boothroyd in a letter to Fleming, as 'a lady's gun, and not a very nice lady at that'. He suggested it had little stopping power and that Bond would be much better served with a revolver such as the Smith & Wesson Centennial Airweight. Fleming thanked Boothroyd for his letter and said he felt Bond ought to have an automatic instead of a revolver, though agreed the Beretta 418 lacked power.

LEFT: Ah, my favourite gadget – the magnetic Rolex. Ideal for deflecting bullets, attracting gas pellets or for unzipping ladies' dresses.

LEFT: Seiko took over as the official Bond watch suppliers in *The Man With The Golden Gun*.

LEFT: A couple of years on, and Seiko were still supplying 007 with their latest watch. It was waterproof.

BELOW: Sometimes the Bond baddies have gadgets too. In *The Man With The Golden Gun* it came in the shape of … yes, you've guessed it, a golden gun. The gun comprised everyday items such as a pen, a cufflink and a cigarette case.

BELOW: The original, made by Pinewood Effects engineer Bert Luxford.

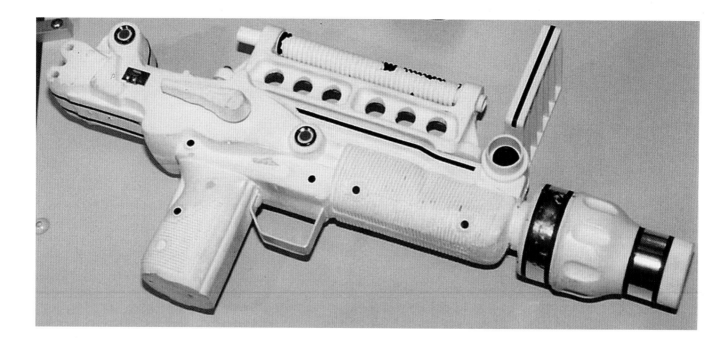

TOP: One of the laser guns we used in our space-fight finale in *Moonraker*.

ABOVE: A handy wrist dart gun, as described by Q in *Moonraker*. Another 'must' for Christmas.

RIGHT: Bond was issued with a new gun in *Tomorrow Never Dies*, a Walther P99, which he kept for the next few adventures.

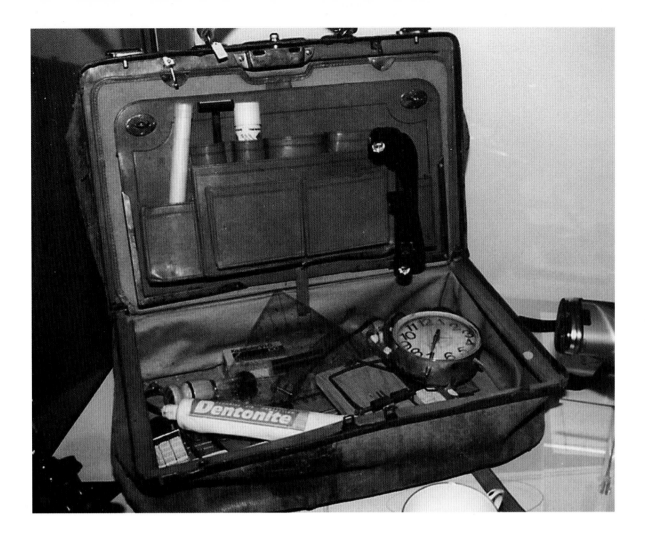

In *Dr. No* Jimmy was hauled in to M's office, where we learned he had carried a Beretta for ten years but, on one assignment, the said pistol – with the suppressor attached – snagged in his waistband. He was hospitalized for six months.

Boothroyd recommended the Walther PPK 7.65 mm as being the best choice for an automatic, with ammunition available everywhere. In thanks to Boothroyd, Fleming later called his armourer Major Boothroyd.

The Walther PPK was presented to Jim in *Dr. No* and was said to have an impact like 'a brick through a plate-glass window'. I used a PPK in all my films, though it fell out of favour with the real Secret Service when, on 20 March 1974, an attempt was made to kidnap HRH Princess Anne. The police officer protecting the princess was carrying a Walther PPK and it jammed. The gun was subsequently withdrawn from use.

In the Pierce Brosnan films the PPK was updated with a Walther P99, but they reverted to a PPK again with Daniel Craig in *Quantum Of Solace*. Whenever I had to fire the PPK, I used to anticipate the 'bang' and blink. The director would call for us to go again, because I often blinked and winced several seconds before I pulled the trigger. Such a coward.

ABOVE: Everything for the traveller abroad – Q's deadly travel kit includes an alarm clock (guaranteed never to awaken the user) and Dentonite toothpaste, the latest in plastic explosive.

ABOVE: A rocket-firing plaster cast. Only Q could come up with such a novelty!

TOP RIGHT: A new Ericsson mobile phone did everything from remotely driving a car to ... making a phone call in *Tomorrow Never Dies*.

BOTTOM RIGHT: Desmond Llewelyn posing as a car rental salesman at Hamburg Airport in *Tomorrow Never Dies*. He had a hard time persuading Pierce Brosnan's Jimmy Bond to take out accident insurance!

EXPLOSIVE FUN

The first real Bond gadget was of course the attaché case in *From Russia With Love*. It contained:

AN AR-7 .22 SURVIVAL RIFLE WITH INFRARED TELESCOPE
50 GOLD SOVEREIGNS
A TEAR GAS CANISTER DISGUISED AS TALCUM POWDER
AMMUNITION FOR RIFLE
A THROWING KNIFE

But should you ever find yourself issued with one, be sure to turn the catches the correct way when opening, or else the tear gas canister will explode in your face.

Terence Young and Peter Hunt decided to have a bit of fun with this element of the case when some United Artists executives were visiting Pinewood. They ran the first couple of reels of the movie, and when it reached the scene where Bond opens the attaché case, Peter cut to the huge explosion from the end of *Dr.*

No and ran the closing titles. The End.

Although he and Terence collapsed in hysterics, the UA execs were not particularly amused. But that was the type of fun you could have on a Bond movie.

In *Goldfinger* a brilliant set of homing beacons was presented to Jim. The first, larger, one was attached to the villain's vehicle and its early GPS-type technology used to locate his Swiss base. The second, smaller one, concealed in Jim's shoe, allowed MI6 to track him. It really was a prototype of GPS as we know it today – and very useful for the likes of jealous wives.

Q came up with some jolly ideas in *Thunderball* – the first time he was sent on location, incidentally, but Desmond couldn't sun himself in the Bahamas for continuity reasons – including the Bell Rocket Belt, which was used to propel Bond into the air when escaping Jacques Bouvar; then there was the Underwater Jet Pack used during the final undersea battle. Most usefully, there was an underwater camera capable of taking eight shots in darkness using an infrared film. We take that sort of thing for granted these days, but back then it was revolutionary.

While in Japan, Jim took full advantage of visiting their version of Q-Branch in *You Only Live Twice*. He marvelled at the mini-rocket cigarette Tiger Tanaka demonstrated – capable of shooting a jet-powered dart accurately up to thirty yards – and quipped, 'This cigarette can really save your life.'

Then there was dear Little Nellie: the Wallis WA-116 Series 1 autogyro, assembled (and disassembled) to fit into several suitcases. Nellie is armed with rocket launchers, air mines, machine guns, rear-mounted flame-throwers and infrared-guided AA smart missiles. The idea for her inclusion came one morning when Ken Adam heard a radio interview with Nellie's inventor, Wing Commander Ken Wallis, saying he'd relish the chance to pit his little autogyro against 'the big boys'. She certainly did him proud in the movie.

When Sean departed the series and George Lazenby stepped in there was a distinct lack of gadgets. Okay, there was radioactive lint, a safe cracker and a prototype Xerox machine, but not much else to excite us technical geeks. Bond was to rely more on his wits than Q-Branch. Wits are good, but gadgets are fun, and thankfully more were in evidence when Sean returned for *Diamonds Are Forever*, which featured the pickpocket's hated snap trap; a fake fingerprint to trick Tiffany Case into believing 007 is Peter Franks; and a voice changer that Blofeld uses to fool employees into thinking he is Willard Whyte and, subsequently, Q uses to fool Blofeld.

The most profitable of all gadgets, however, was a little ring that prompted every fruit machine to pay out a jackpot. Desmond said he collected up hundreds of dollars' worth of coins from the machines when the scene was completed, and decided rather than take them home he'd feed them back in to win an even bigger jackpot. Alas, the F/X guys had long gone home and the magic ring was of no use ... he lost the lot!

LEFT: A handy set of folding pocket binoculars.

BELOW LEFT: In order to identify a few people in *A View To A Kill*, Jim is issued with a miniature camera cunningly hidden in his signet ring.

BELOW: One of Q's new toys in *A View To A Kill* was a remote-controlled surveillance device called SNOOPER.

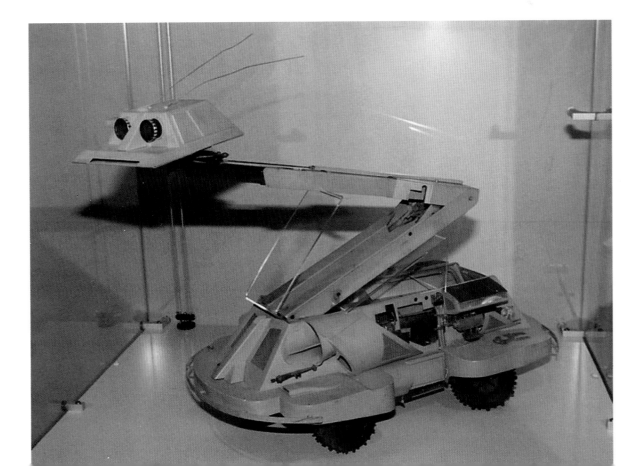

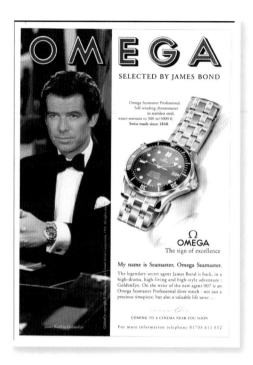

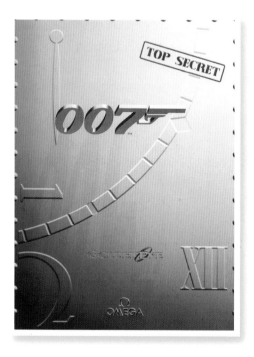

TIME TO PLAY

But more lovely toys were to come when yours truly stepped into the role in 1973. Apart from the Bug Sweeper, a Clothing Brush Communicator, a Shark gun that fired special highly pressurized air pellets and a genuine 'Felix Lighter' radio transmitter/receiver, there was a brilliant state-of-the-art Pulsar watch that illuminated to show the digital clock face.

There was also a lovely Rolex Submariner given to Bond by Moneypenny, after being repaired by Q. This was no ordinary watch. It featured a powerful electromagnet that was said to be able to deflect a bullet. More importantly, it could be used to unzip a lady's dress. I was ever so disappointed when the F/X boys said it didn't really work, and that Derek Meddings would instead have his hand up Maddy Smith's skirt, pulling the zip down using a piece of wire. Lucky old Derek. Constant retakes did mean I got to spend the whole day with dear Maddy, perfecting my technique. Ah, if only I could find a working prototype of that watch today ... I could give Maddy a call to see if she fancied re-enacting the scene. The Submariner also featured a spinning bezel that acted as a rotating saw, enabling Jim to cut his rope restraints and escape a pool full of man-eating sharks and then go on and rescue Solitaire.

Did I ever get to keep any of the gadgets, is something I'm often asked. Alas no, they were whisked from set as soon as filming ended for the day. Shame, as I could earn a nice pension on eBay.

In my second outing, it was the villainous Francisco Scaramanga who had the great gadgets. His legendary Golden Gun was assembled from a pen (the barrel) inserted into a cigarette case (the firing chamber), a cigarette lighter (the handle), and a cufflink (the trigger). This gun is limited to just one golden bullet, which are all handcrafted by speciality munitions manufacturer Lazar – they are all 4.2 mm (an unusual size) and made of twenty-three-carat gold. The bullets flatten upon impact.

In *The Spy Who Loved Me* I of course had the wonderful Lotus Esprit and all its gadgets, but in addition was issued with a handy ski-pole-cum-gun, modified to fire .30-calibre rounds from a four-shot magazine in the handle. I saw Michael Billington off with that.

Then there was a Seiko Quartz watch. It was the second film to feature the brand after a major tie-in for *The Man With The Golden Gun*, but this was the first film in which it had a purpose – a ticker-tape pager that allowed MI6 to send important messages to Jim. The Seiko was back in *Moonraker*, though this time with the added bonus of a high explosive charge and remote detonator incorporated. It accompanied the wrist dart gun, capable of firing both cyanide-coated and armour-piercing darts. Jim used that to save himself from an out-of-control centrifuge simulator and then kill Hugo Drax. It's never a good idea to get into an out-of-control centrifuge simulator without one, let me tell you.

I was also armed with a safe-cracking device concealed within a cigarette case; a mini-camera imprinted with 007; and a laser gun. Oh, and I stole a poison pen from CIA agent Holly Goodhead's toys. Bond used this particular gadget to dispose of Drax's pet python. I think when you have to act alongside a twelve-foot-long rubber snake – and try to appear more animated than it – you know you've cracked this acting lark.

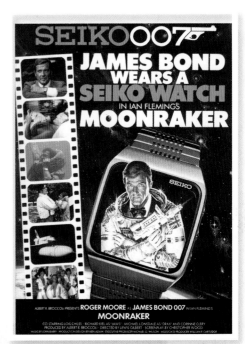

FABERGÉ EGGS TO FAKE CROCS

My trusty Seiko survived to accompany me in *For Your Eyes Only*, where it received digital message read-outs and operated as a two-way radio/transmitter for voice communications, much to the Prime Minister's surprise.

The main object of the film's story was to locate and retrieve the Automatic Targeting Attack Communicator (ATAC), which had been lost when the British spy ship *St Georges* was sunk. This device controlled all of Britain's Polaris nuclear submarines and

TOP: Seiko were with us again on this one.

ABOVE: My flexible friend. Handy for opening any lock, and paying for lunch, too.

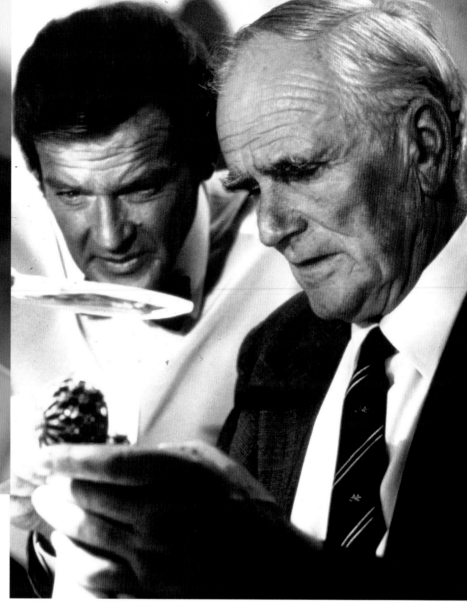

ABOVE AND RIGHT: In *Octopussy*, Q fixed a listening and homing device inside the Fabergé egg.

could either render them inoperative or coordinate them against major Western cities or, heaven forbid, against Britain herself. In its pursuit I helped Q load up the Identigraph device to assemble a photo of our suspect by selecting characteristics from a variety of lists including hair colour, hairstyle, nose form, style of eyeglasses etc. Poor Desmond Llewelyn had terrible trouble setting up the machine and remembering his complicated lines, so I took over the technical end and it worked rather well.

When *Octopussy* came around, the Seiko graduated to containing a universal radio direction finder, working in conjunction with a listening device inside Bond's fountain pen and the fake Fabergé egg. I also employed loaded backgammon dice – though not in my games with Cubby – and a Mont Blanc fountain pen that contained a mixture of nitric and hydrochloric acids. Have you seen the price of refills for those things?

One of the fun gadgets – or is it a mode of transport? – was the 'fake crocodile', actually a miniature motorboat used to get Jimmy to Octopussy's Island. I bravely climbed into it for the close-ups, but allowed Paul Weston to drive it in the scene, just in case a *real* frisky crocodile wandered into shot. That might have been tricky!

In my last outing as Jim I was armed with all manner of useful gizmos. There were polarizing sunglasses that let Jim see clearly through tinted glass; a ring containing a miniature camera; a billfold that used ultraviolet light to read previously written material by picking up the indentations of pen marks on paper; a bug detector contained within an electric razor; a credit card for popping open locked windows; a tracking device to locate a stolen microchip buried in the snow; and, of course, SNOOPER – one of Q's surveillance inventions in the form of a small, animal-like remote-controlled camera that can transmit audio/video.

ABOVE: An innocent-looking pair of CK glasses. But touch a switch and it sets off a detonator in Jim's P99 gun.

BELOW: This innocent-looking electric shaver is actually a sophisticated bug detector in *A View To A Kill.*

GADGET HEAVEN

After my tenure as 007 ended, Q stayed on to look after Timothy Dalton and Pierce Brosnan. Their haul of gadgets was ever impressive and ingenious. In *The Living Daylights* Q produced a Philips Keychain, which had become widely popular in locating lost keys. However, Q's contained some non-standard extras, including a capsule of stun gas, activated by the first bars of 'Rule, Britannia', and an explosive charge set off by a wolf whistle! The keychain also featured a lock-pick, effective on ninety per cent of the world's locks …

In his second film with Timothy Dalton, Q found himself in the field and carried a bag of everyday travel items including

ABOVE: Q with my successor, Timothy Dalton, who was receiving a briefing on the key finder, which was operated by a whistle.

RIGHT: Of course there were toy guns produced to tie in with the films. They came in all shapes and sizes.

Dentonite Toothpaste – actually plastic explosive with the detonator disguised as a packet of cigarettes. There was also a wonderful gun that could be programmed to fire for only one person, and an exploding alarm clock – guaranteed never to wake up anyone who uses it.

When Pierce donned the famous tuxedo it was accompanied by a leather belt that concealed a piton capable of firing up to seventy-five feet of high-tensile wire, that could take the weight of an average person. Then there was a Parker pen for his top pocket that contained a class-four grenade. A new wristwatch in the shape of Omega Seamaster Professional – with laser cutter and remote detonator – completed the ensemble.

When *Tomorrow Never Dies* came around, the burgeoning mobile-phone market was tapped and Ericsson supplied a concept model loaded with a variety of features, including a 20,000-volt stun gun, and a nifty fingerprint analyser. The best feature in my view was the remote control for Jimmy's BMW – a masterpiece that no agent should be without.

With the fortieth anniversary of the films in 2002, the producers decided it was time to pay homage to some of the gadgets laid up in storage from the previous twenty films and have Bond wander around them, picking up a wristwatch (with explosive detonator and laser cutter) and a ring that can shatter bulletproof glass.

Since *Casino Royale* in 2006, the character of Q and his lab have been absent from the films. While Bond is still outfitted with a number of gadgets, they seem less futuristic and awe-inspiring and are based on technology already commercially available rather than Q's flights of fancy. The cellphones are smarter – the one in *Quantum Of Solace* had an identification imager that could compile a composite facial image. I wonder if that was on contract or pay-as-you-go?

One thing that is constant is Jimmy's love of a good watch – and let's face it, it's his watch that has got him out of several nasty situations. I used to wear an Omega all the time, and still do wear my limited-edition Submariner on occasion, but my main timepiece is a Breitling, which I used in a commercial for the Hanson Trust in Ireland. After the third and last day of filming, I asked my son Christian (who was assistant director) to take it back to the production office.

'No, keep it, it's yours,' he said. There was no way I was going to pinch a £5,000 watch!

'No,' he said, 'Kristina saw you admiring it and has bought it for you.'

My wife also bought me a Piaget watch, which I use when in formalwear as it's very lightweight and thin. My wife, as well as having great taste, is also very generous.

ABOVE AND BELOW: Omega remained Jimbo's watch of choice throughout Pierce's tenure – and still features with Daniel in the role.

BOND
ON
CARS

BOND ON CARS

PREVIOUS PAGES: Daniel Craig continues to be a safe driver and I believe he took out accidental damage insurance in case of a dent or scratch.

As well as gadgets, of course, Q has supplied 007 with cars for many decades now. Jimmy has driven his fair share of models: Bentley … Ford … GM … Aston Martin … Mercedes-Benz … BMW … Lotus … Rolls-Royce … Citröen … Renault. All were internationally recognized makers of motorcars and all have benefited hugely from the exposure.

PETROL HEADS UNITE!

It was a different story when I was making a TV series called *The Saint*. We thought it would be rather good if Simon Templar drove a British Jaguar car and our production manager, Johnny Goodman, duly approached them about a twenty-six-part primetime TV show. 'Oh, and we need three … next week.'

They shrugged their shoulders in a rather pompous way. 'Think of the publicity!' Johnny exclaimed. They told Johnny they

BELOW: It wasn't really until *Goldfinger* that the 'Bond car' really grabbed people's imagination. The Aston Martin DB5 featured a wealth of optional extras.

LEFT: The gear knob triggered an ejector seat, there was an early GPS tracking monitor, weapons tray, front-firing machine guns, mud slick, rear bulletproof screen and more.

RIGHT: Oh yes, it also had revolving number plates inspired by director Guy Hamilton getting fed up of receiving parking tickets in London.

BELOW: The Bond DB5 even had its own specification booklet.

TOP SECRET

Specification of the James Bond Aston Martin

had order books bulging and a waiting list they couldn't fulfil as it was ... 'Why do we need publicity?'

So we went to Volvo, who couldn't do enough to help us. Volvo is still going strong ... and Jaguar? Well, they're around.

As 007 I have found myself at the wheel of many modes of vehicular transport; however, as my friend Michael Caine might say 'not a lot of people know that ...' The Bamford & Martin 1.5-litre Side Valve Short Chassis Tourer was James Bond's very first car.

According to the first 'Young Bond' book, *SilverFin*, by Charlie Higson, Jimmy inherited the car at the age of thirteen from his uncle Max, and drove it regularly, even though he was underage. The car was destroyed in the third Young Bond novel, *Double or Die*, leading Bond to replace it with the Bentley Mark IV – as later featured in Fleming's novels, although petrol heads among you will know there has never been a Bentley model known as the 'Mark IV'. That appellation was a creation of Ian Fleming, and erroneously perpetuated ever since.

James Bond's car in the Ian Fleming novels was a grey 1933 Bentley convertible – featuring a 4.5-litre engine with the Amherst Villiers supercharger. Unlike in the films, no gadgets were ever installed in the cars Bond used in Fleming's novels. The only armament mentioned at all was a .45 Colt Army Special revolver that Jim kept in the glove compartment.

The Bentley was actually the very first Bond car seen in the film series, shown briefly during *From Russia With Love* in the scene with Jimmy and Sylvia Trench alongside the River Thames. It featured the added extra of a car phone, which in 1963 was – like many other Bond gadgets – a prototype for future developments.

In *Goldfinger* Bond asks about his Bentley in Q-Branch, only to be told that it has 'had its day' and is instead presented with an

Aston Martin DB5 – perhaps the car most famously associated with the entire 007 series. To date the model has featured in five films – *Goldfinger, Thunderball, GoldenEye, Tomorrow Never Dies* and *Casino Royale*. I'm told it was also due to feature in *The World Is Not Enough*, but the shots of it being driven were cut. The 2006 reboot of the series showed Bond winning it in a game of poker in the Bahamas – without any special extras.

DB OR NOT DB?

Though I never drove an Aston Martin as Bond, I did drive a DB5 in the comedy film *The Cannonball Run*, and a DBS in *The Persuaders!*. The DB5 also popped up in the TV film *The Return of the Man from U.N.C.L.E.*, with George Lazenby playing a character called 'JB'.

The DB5 car as used in *Goldfinger* and *Thunderball* was the prototype model, with another standard car (later modified) used for stunts. Both cars were loaned to Eon Productions for the duration of filmmaking and later for publicity tours. Two further cars were later purchased and 'adapted' for promotional use through to the late 1960s, one of which sold in 2006 for $2,090,000 (approximately £1.4 million); the second is in the Louwman Collection Museum in the Netherlands. The original gadget car, meanwhile, was stripped of its accessories and sold as a standard car, only to be retrofitted by the purchaser. It was mysteriously stolen in 1997 and has never been found. The second 'original'

TOP: Corgi launched its most successful ever film tie-in model with the DB5 and has since sold over seven million units.

ABOVE: And it still sells today!

ABOVE LEFT: Desmond Llewelyn and Honor Blackman at the launch of the new Corgi range of Bond models in the mid-1990s.

ABOVE RIGHT: Prince Andrew was given a fully operational scale model of a DB5 for his sixth birthday.

DB5 was sold in 2010, for £2.6 million.

The famous scene in which Q demonstrates all the car's gadgets to Bond was not originally in the script. Desmond finished his day's filming and returned home. Cubby called him. He'd been thinking: demonstrating the gadgets to Bond would surely heighten the audience's excitement to see them in action. As the set was still in place, would Desmond come in for a second day of filming?

Gadgets fitted for *Goldfinger* include …

- Front-firing Browning .30-calibre machine guns behind the front indicators
- Retractable tyre-slashing blades concealed in the rear wheel hub caps
- Radio telephone in the driver's door panel
- Radar scanner and tracking screen hidden behind car radio speaker
- Passenger ejector seat
- Oil slick spray hidden within rear light cluster
- Caltrop ejector device hidden within rear light cluster
- Smoke screen from exhaust pipes
- Front and rear extending rams
- Gun cabinet under driver's seat
- Bulletproof windscreen and rising bulletproof rear screen
- Revolving number plates, valid all countries, naturally:
    BMT 216A (UK)   4711-EA-62 (France)   LU 6789 (Switzerland)

Other Astons featured in the series include:

❦ A DBS was used in the pre-credits and closing scenes of *On Her Majesty's Secret Service* as Jim and Tracy's wedding car. It was glimpsed in the subsequent film, *Diamonds Are Forever*, parked up in Q-Branch.

❦ In *The Living Daylights* Timothy Dalton drove a V8 Vantage Volante convertible and its hardtop version. All the usual refinements were in place, including extending side outriggers, spike-producing tyres, missiles, lasers, signal-intercepting smart radio, head-up display and rocket propulsion. It could also self-destruct when primed. Doesn't every car?

❦ Pierce Brosnan's first outing as 007 – *GoldenEye* – brought back the Aston Martin DB5 and this time pitted it against a Ferrari in the hills above Monte Carlo; while in his last outing, *Die Another Day*, the Aston Martin V12 Vanquish (or 'Vanish') was introduced by the new Q. It featured front-firing rockets, hood-mounted target-seeking guns, spike-producing tyres and a passenger ejector seat in homage to the original Aston Martin DB5. This Aston was also equipped with 'adaptive camouflage' – a cloaking device that allowed it to become effectively invisible at the push of a button. Hmmmm. A little far-fetched even for Bond!

❦ When *Casino Royale* hit the screens, we saw the new Aston Martin DBS V1 (right) as Jim's car of choice, although no special gadgets were visible other than the compartments that housed his Walther P99 and an emergency medical kit. It turned up again in *Quantum Of Solace* and was all but destroyed after a chase in Siena, Italy. Nice to know some things don't change.

ABOVE: Special-effects engineer Bert Luxford with his adapted BSA motorcycle for *Thunderball*.

BELOW: The DB5 returns in *Casino Royale*.

TOP LEFT: Little Nellie, the autogyro, held her honour against several SPECTRE airborne thugs in *You Only Live Twice*.

LEFT: And here is her 'Uncle', dear Desmond Llewelyn, describing her operation to 007 – please note he is wearing shorts!

TOP RIGHT: And here she is today, still proudly sporting her 007 weaponry.

ESPRIT DE CORPS!

My own Bondmobile came in the shape of the Lotus Esprit. The story goes that Donovan McLauchlan, public relations manager at Lotus, had been tipped off that the next Bond movie, *The Spy Who Loved Me,* was gearing up for pre-production at Pinewood. It was early 1976, and he drove an Esprit to the studios and parked it right in the path of anyone trying to get in or out of the main admin building entrance. It wasn't long before Cubby saw the car and made a phone call – not to get it towed, but to ask all about it. Their gamble paid off.

Lotus loaned us two production Esprit's, five Esprit body shells and two Lotus personnel for the shoot. The body shells were used to make the underwater car, as adapted by Perry Oceanographics. A full underwater conversion mode with fins, front-mounted rocket launchers, mines, a periscope, a smoke screen and a surface-to-air missile was pretty exciting. There was also a cement sprayer concealed behind the registration plates.

Other body shells were used in various scenes, including the shot of the Esprit driving off the pier into the sea. That one was powered by compressed air, equipped with a space-frame and locked steering wheel … It's nice to know no actors were harmed.

Lotus sales increased dramatically after the film's release, with a

ABOVE: The Corgi model of the Lotus Esprit.

BELOW: Just popping into the cove for its 6,000-mile service.

ABOVE: Always room for a
pretty passenger in the Lotus
Esprit.

three-year waiting list for Esprits in particular. I myself was offered the opportunity to buy one at a ten per cent discount. Needless to say, their overwhelming generosity was not something that particularly excited me.

The cars were problematic in the extreme. During filming, their engines overheated and batteries ran down quickly. Their low driving position made elegant exits from the car an issue, and all this made the action location in Sardinia a little fraught.

When we heard later that publicist John Willis was due to drive the car from London to the Cannes Film Festival in May 1977, we took bets on whether he'd make it. He did get as far as Lyon without issue, before ending up on the back of a tow truck heading for a local garage. It then limped into Cannes, was positioned outside the Carlton Hotel and duly refused to move again thanks to a flat battery. If only the world's press could have snapped the team of mechanics at work during the dead of night, it would have made terrific headlines – 'James Bond's car breaks down'.

Though the Lotus transformed into a submarine on screen, a combination of miniatures and body shells were used to achieve the effect of the conversion. It could be driven underwater, but only in a full wetsuit, as the interior was not air-locked. Consequently it was dubbed 'Wet Nellie'.

The scene where the car emerges from the ocean onto a beach, was shot in two parts: with an Esprit shell being pulled on a tow rope to the point at which the car was to emerge, and then a cut to the real car in the surf. The little toddler who watches the car come out of the water and points is Richard Kiel's son, RJ. He's now a thirty-six-year-old doctor.

I thought it might be a giggle to wind down the window and drop a fish out as we drove onto the beach. Cubby wasn't at all happy, and said we should re-shoot; he felt it was a little too flippant and therefore not funny. I said OK, but when we ran both versions in rushes the next day my prank got a huge laugh. Cubby conceded.

In *For Your Eyes Only* the Lotus returned, twice. The first one, a white Esprit Turbo, was destroyed when a thug tripped its self-destruct system by breaking the driver's-side window. The second one, a red version of the same model, was driven by *moi* in Northern Italy, though you didn't get to see many of the gadgets in operation, I'm afraid, as a wonderful scene with John Moreno as Luigi – where he tampered with a few buttons – was unfortunately cut due to time constraints. If you listen carefully, when I leave him in the car to go into the ice rink I tell him not to play with any of the buttons.

BELOW: Cubby really didn't like my little joke of dropping a fish out of the window when we emerged from the sea. However, when it got more laughs than the scripted version in rushes, he conceded it was one of my better ideas.

OVER AIR, LAND AND SEA

The wet bike was another brilliant innovation first seen by the public in a Bond movie – again, in *For Your Eyes Only*. I was given a little time to get used to it on the beach at the Cala di Volpe and, in my bathing trunks, leapt aboard and mastered the controls, swishing around in the surf thinking it was all rather like a jet boat. Then I was told in the scene I'd be wearing full Naval Commander uniform for the ride to Stromberg's lair, and I had to arrive immaculate and dry, without a hair out of place. OK, I thought, I'll give it a whirl.

ABOVE: The Glastron boat chase in *Live And Let Die* was, thankfully, filmed at the beginning of the production schedule. I'd hurt my leg in rehearsals and could happily sit down for my brave introduction as 007.

Fresh from the hair-and-make-up truck, I hopped onto the bike, started her up and made my way out to sea. It was all perfectly fine until I heard the 'chop-chop-chop' of the helicopter above, obviously filming. Just then, a huge downdraft created by its rotors took hold and started pushing the bike down into the sea. I had no way of contacting either the helicopter or the boat behind, but knew if I fell in it would mean a complete wardrobe change, hair, make-up, the lot – and that would take a very long time. More by steely determination and grit than anything else I managed to keep the bike going at no more than a forty-five-degree angle to the surface. Sometimes being brave is pretty tough going.

As well as kitting Bond out with the best thing on four wheels, the writers sometimes turn an idea on its head and say, 'Let's try him in a ...' Well, if a Lotus is one of the most powerful cars, the direct opposite would be a Citroën 2CV, with its mere two-horsepower engine, yet another vehicle that featured in *For Your Eyes Only*. It was huge fun to drive down through olive groves in – it just goes to show, it's more about the driver's skill than it is the size of his engine, or so the Bond girls say.

But what on earth could be even less powerful than a 2CV? How about an Indian Tuk-Tuk motorized rickshaw?

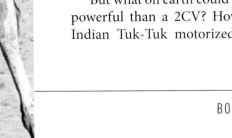

With the pull of a lawnmower engine, and manoeuvrability of same, it was used to great effect in *Octopussy* as an escape vehicle.

Oh, and I shouldn't forget the 'Bondola' from *Moonraker*. That was all rather tongue-in-cheek, but why wouldn't Jim have a supercharged gondola? Filming in Venice is never particularly easy, especially with the vast crowds looking on, but shooting around the canals was fairly straightforward as there was nowhere for people to watch – aside from a few bridges – and it all happened so fast, they didn't really know what it was all about anyway as we were there under stealth.

ABOVE LEFT: By land, by sea and then by air ... if I'm not mistaken it was the first time we saw Jimmy hang-glide into the villain's lair. I was so brave.

ABOVE RIGHT: In *The Man With The Golden Gun* it wasn't just Jimmy who had a gadget car. Villain Scaramanga (Christopher Lee) owned a Matador Coupé, which converted into a flying car.

FAR LEFT: Not the most gadget-packed of Bond vehicles ... I think he got the hump with me.

LEFT: The tipping Bondola from *Moonraker*. Lucky I had my little hooter to warn passersby to move out of the way.

ABOVE: Don't fall off! I knew if I did I'd face a two-mile trip back to shore for make-up, hair and new costume.

BELOW: From the sublime to the ridiculous, a two-horsepower getaway vehicle in *For Your Eyes Only*.

Once we reached St Mark's Square for the scene where the gondola converts into a hovercraft, however, we were confronted with 20,000–30,000 tourists, largely Oriental, all armed with Nikon cameras.

There were two gondolas used in the sequence: the first inflated and raised out of the water, then we cut to a second on land, which was built around a Ford chassis. I arrived in my lovely light-grey silk suit for the first take, sat in the boat and the air was switched on – but seemingly only on one side, thus toppling me out and straight into the Grand Canal. Cue much laughter and snapping of Nikons. I trotted off to dry, change, have my hair and make-up done and, thirty minutes later, returned.

'Action!' called Lewis, and I was tipped sideways into the canal yet again. This happened on five takes, where one side inflated faster than the other, tipping me in each time. Each time, the laughter increased, as did the size of the crowds gathered. Take 6 – and my final dry suit. Thankfully, it worked and we wrapped for the day.

Next morning, I hopped inside the Ford-chassis gondola to drive it right the way across the square, which by then was starting to fill with tourists. Rather than attempt to control the crowds, Lewis said we'd just shoot, as they really wouldn't know what we were doing until it was over.

'Fair enough,' I said. 'But I really do feel I need some sort of horn to warn people that there is a motorized gondola approaching

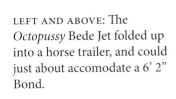

LEFT AND ABOVE: The *Octopussy* Bede Jet folded up into a horse trailer, and could just about accomodate a 6' 2" Bond.

them, driven by an English actor, on St Mark's Square as it's not something they'd really expect.' They found some sort of claxon, and I literally beep-beeped my way around unsuspecting tourists, across to a sharp right turn down a narrow road. It was so narrow the F/X boys put Vaseline down the side of the gondola so I could slip down more easily.

Then of course in *Live And Let Die* I took it to another extreme when I drove an AEC Regent RT-type double-decker bus. I remember that day well: it was 7 December 1972, on location in Montego Bay, Jamaica, and I had to drive it under a low bridge, sheering off the top deck. Maurice Patchett from London Transport's Chiswick depot spent three months preparing for the stunt, including taking me on a crash course – forgive the pun – on the Chiswick skid pad. Maurice took over the driving as the bus headed for the bridge; the top deck had been carefully removed and replaced only on rollers, to ensure a relatively clean detachment as it hit at precisely 30 mph.

Maurice said that if the film game didn't work out for me, I'd make a good London bus man. That would have pleased my

ABOVE: On location in Paris for *A View To A Kill*, I had to drive and virtually destroy a Renault taxi in my pursuit of Mayday. I guess it beats having to tip a driver.

mum, who still lived in hope I might one day get a proper job.

I also chopped the top of a car off in a film – a Renault 11 taxi in fact – in the Parisian scenes of *A View To A Kill*, while trying to chase Grace Jones. Wish I hadn't bothered trying, actually. Nevertheless, that was a terrific sequence, all very carefully orchestrated by the superb Remy Julienne. Alas, these days when visiting Paris I have to sit in the traffic just like everyone else.

In my last 007 outing, I found myself at the controls of a San Francisco fire truck. When I heard we were going to be shooting in the city, I thought, 'Oh, here we go, another attempt at bettering *Bullit* with Steve McQueen,' but when they told me my mode of transport would be somewhat different, I was intrigued. It certainly cleared the traffic off the roads.

And just to prove Q didn't exclusively think of the 00 section in his work, he designed himself a fishing boat – for his retirement. The Q-boat came equipped with submersible capabilities, torpedoes, rocket booster and GPS tracking, though Q was keen to point out it was not properly finished when Jim took off in it during *The World Is Not Enough*.

THE CLASSIC STUNT

I can't end any discussion of Bond cars and assorted vehicles without mentioning the AMC Hornet, can I? The what? Well, if I was to say when Jim is chasing Mary Goodnight in *The Man With The Golden Gun*, he steals a car in which Sheriff J.W. Pepper is about to take a test drive, you'll be with me. During the chase, Jim makes a corkscrew jump over a river. That wasn't just lucky guesswork, but the first case of a computer designing a stunt. Race car driver Jay Milligan, who promoted the American Thrill Show during the 1960s and 1970s, first performed the stunt, known as the Astro Spiral Jump, on 12 January 1972 at the Houston Astrodome. Always keen to hear about anything a bit unusual or daring, Cubby was soon told about the stunt everyone was talking about, and put a call through to Milligan.

Researchers at Cornell University for the National Highway Traffic Safety Administration did a computer simulation of the stunt to calculate the exact angles required, speeds to drive and so forth. These details were passed over to the production team, and the bridge was erected.

With Milligan supervising, the 360-degree spiral was shot in just one take, with British stuntman 'Bumps' Williard at the wheel and with eight cameras simultaneously capturing the action. Meanwhile divers, ambulances and cranes were on standby in case of any unforeseen consequences. The jump was over in a second and to achieve greater screen time is shown in slow motion. Williard was given a large bonus for completing it on the first take, by the way.

ABOVE: The opening of *GoldenEye* saw new 007 Pierce Brosnan chase a plane down a runway on a motorbike. As you do.

BELOW: The AMC Hornet that performed the amazing 360-degree roll in *The Man With The Golden Gun*.

RIGHT: When Q retired, he envisaged a life of fishing. So he built himself a fishing boat – albeit with missiles, GPS and other gadgets. Perhaps to help land those big catches?

MIDDLE RIGHT: Though sometimes, when a BMW or Aston is not available, a smaller mode of transport will suffice.

BELOW: With *Die Another Day* the Aston Martin was back, in the shape of the Vanquish – or Vanish, as 007 dubbed it.

FAR RIGHT TOP: And here is the Vanquish in action!

FAR RIGHT BOTTOM: With Daniel Craig, a new Aston Martin was introduced – the DB9. Something tells me he'll have to go for the expensive valeting option.

BOND
ON
STYLE

BOND ON STYLE

Once upon a time, heroes wore chainmail and armour, rode around on horses and sat down to an opulent banquet using their bare hands to tear apart their food. That wouldn't do for Jimmy Bond – the quintessential well-dressed English spy who epitomizes style. Old Jimbo has become something of a style icon and the phrase 'living the Bond lifestyle' conjures up images of the very best things life has to offer by way of sharp clothes, expensive champagnes, fast cars, beautiful women, speed boats and fine dining.

Bond preferred Polish or Russian vodka at a time when the only brand available in the West would have been Stolichnaya. Besides his famous 'Martini, shaken, not stirred', Jim often drank

PREVIOUS PAGES: Sharing a glass of bubbly in Chantilly with Tania Roberts.

LEFT: The famous vodka Martini, so often stirred instead of being shaken. Although I never ordered one in any of my seven films, here I am with one – though not, I hasten to add, served in a proper Martini glass.

BELOW: Mention the 'Bond lifestyle' and images of casinos, fast cars, speedboats and beautiful girls all come to mind, as is so brilliantly illustrated in this competition flyer from 1989.

ABOVE: Variation on a theme – Daniel Craig enjoys a Vesper Martini with Eva Green – aka Vesper – in *Casino Royale*. When Vesper asks Bond if he named the drink after her because of the bitter aftertaste, 007 replies that he named it for her, 'because once you have tasted it, you won't drink anything else.'

a shot of straight vodka, served with a pinch of black pepper. This was not for the flavour, he explained, 'but because it caused the impurities in cheap vodka to sink to the bottom'. Though I fear that trick wouldn't have improved the Siamese vodka he downed in the film *You Only Live Twice*!

Bond and vodka have gone hand in hand since *Dr. No*, when the titular villain handed 007 a 'Martini, shaken not stirred'. This fleeting moment in the film literally changed the way Martini drinkers made their cocktails from then on, shifting from the traditional gin to a vodka-based drink and popularizing the vodka Martini the world over.

I myself prefer a gin Martini and, in all my years of travelling, believe the best is served in the bar of Maison Pic, in Valence, France. How do they prepare it?

First, the ingredients. My gin of choice is Tanqueray and vermouth has to be Noilly Prat.

Take the glass or cocktail shaker you are using and, for two sensible-sized Martinis, fill ¼ of each glass with Noilly Prat. Swill it around and then discard it. Next, top the glasses up with gin, drop in a zest of lemon, and place the glasses in a freezer or ice-cold fridge until you are – or should I say *she* is – ready.

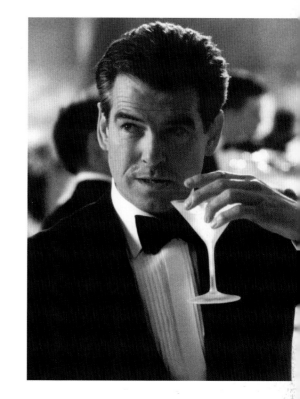

ABOVE AND BELOW: Both Pierce and Timothy were partial to a Martini – but Timothy appears to be mixing his drinks in this shot.

MARTINI IS NOT THE ONLY DRINK ...

Bond appreciates other drinks, too. For instance, when, in my first 007 film, I walked into a Harlem bar, it wasn't a vodka Martini I asked for. Far from it. I requested 'bourbon and water, please – no ice'. In *GoldenEye* Jim drinks a bourbon – Jack Daniel's – with M, while in *The World Is Not Enough* and *Die Another Day* he also enjoys drinking Talisker whisky. M pours Bond a glass of Talisker in *The World Is Not Enough*, into which Bond puts ice – something not at all recommended by the distiller – but his fingers, wet from the ice, exude a fizzing substance, which leads him to realize a bomb had been planted in Sir Robert King's money, money that he'd just been handling. Good old Jim.

But Bond is perhaps more closely associated with the finest champagne – be it served in bed with a delicious girl, in an underwater escape pod or on the way back from the Arctic Circle in a submarine. Most famously Bollinger and Dom Perignon have featured in the movies, though I must admit I have a fondness for Taittinger and am not opposed to Moët & Chandon either.

ABOVE: You can't have a vodka Martini without vodka. Jim preferred Russian. I'm not averse to it, or taking part in a bit of product placement – as seen here in *A View To A Kill*.

Bollinger champagnes used in the movies:

- ❦ *Live And Let Die*: Bollinger
- ❦ Moonraker: Bollinger RD '69
- ❦ *A View To A Kill*: Bollinger '75
- ❦ *Licence To Kill*: Bollinger RD '75
- ❦ *The Living Daylights*: Bollinger …
- ❦ *GoldenEye*: Bollinger Grande Année 1988
- ❦ *Tomorrow Never Dies*: Bollinger Grande Année 1989
- ❦ *The World Is Not Enough*: Bollinger Grande Année 1990
- ❦ *Die Another Day*: Bollinger '61
- ❦ *Casino Royale*: Bollinger Grande Année 1990

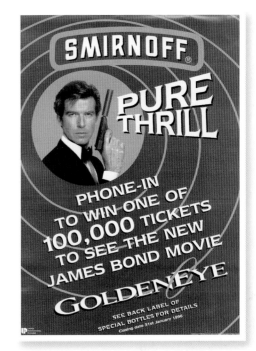

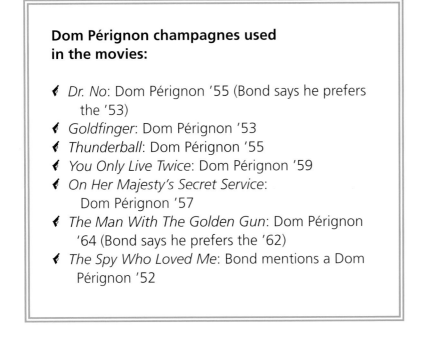

Dom Pérignon champagnes used in the movies:

- *Dr. No*: Dom Pérignon '55 (Bond says he prefers the '53)
- *Goldfinger*: Dom Pérignon '53
- *Thunderball*: Dom Pérignon '55
- *You Only Live Twice*: Dom Pérignon '59
- *On Her Majesty's Secret Service*: Dom Pérignon '57
- *The Man With The Golden Gun*: Dom Pérignon '64 (Bond says he prefers the '62)
- *The Spy Who Loved Me*: Bond mentions a Dom Pérignon '52

Man cannot live by bourbon or champagne alone, however, and so there are also some fine wines served and consumed throughout Jim's adventures, along with some less memorable ones – Phuyuck anyone?

In *Goldfinger*, Bond shows off his sommelier skills to M when brandy is served: 'I'd say it was a thirty-year-old fined and indifferently blended, with an overdose of *bon bois*.'

In Japan for *You Only Live Twice* Jim displays his appreciation of the local rice wine drink when Tiger Tanaka offers him the choice of a vodka Martini or sake. 'Oh no, I like sake, especially when it's served at the correct temperature, 98.4 Fahreneit, like this is.' Hang fire, Jimmy!

My wife Kristina and I discovered the true joy of sake when we were in Japan and Korea, where it is, in fact, served cold. There are two basic types of sake: *Futsū-shu*, which is termed 'ordinary' sake, and *Tokutei meishō-shu*, which is 'special-designation' sake. *Futsū-shu* is the equivalent of table wine and accounts for the majority of sake produced, whereas *Tokutei meishō-shu* denotes the premium sakes, distinguished by the degree to which the rice has been polished and the added percentage of brewer's alcohol or the absence of such additives.

I became a bit of an aficionado, as you can tell. And Jimmy, I have to tell you, hot sake is usually only served as a winter drink, and high-grade sake is *never* served hot because the flavours and aromas are lost.

TOP AND ABOVE: Product placement is a big part of the Bond PR machine.

ABOVE: Shirley Eaton enjoys a glass of champers with Sean Connery in *Goldfinger*. Dom Pérignon '53 I believe?

BELOW: Phuyuck – I'll take a case for Christmas.

A couple of films later, in *Diamonds Are Forever*, it is sherry that becomes the talking point of a meal. Bond, M and Sir Donald Munger (played by my old friend Laurence Naismith, from *The Persuaders!*) are being served the Spanish fortified wine.

'Pity about your liver, sir, it's an unusually fine solera. Fifty-one I believe,' says our hero.

'There is no year for sherry, 007,' replies M.

Not to be outdone, Jim retorts, 'I was referring to the original vintage on which the sherry is based: 1851, unless I'm mistaken?'

Of course he wasn't and a decent knowledge of wines can – literally – save your life. Look at how Red Grant gave himself away in *From Russia With Love* by ordering red wine with fish. Unthinkable! (But possible!)

At the climax of *Diamonds Are Forever*, posing as stewards, the limp-wristed Wint and Kidd give themselves away similarly when they offer Bond a Mouton Rothschild '55. The steward uses a gas ejector to remove the cork – they were all the fashion at one point, even on aeroplanes, until the pressurized gas within caused huge problems with exploding champagne bottles at 30,000 feet – and gives it to Bond, who smells the cork and also gets a whiff of the steward's strong

(and familiar) cologne, and realizes it's the bad guy.

Steward: 'A fine selection, if I may say.'

Bond: 'I'll be the judge of that ... The wine is quite excellent, although for such a grand meal I had rather expected a claret.'

Steward: 'Of course. Unfortunately, our cellar's rather poorly stocked with clarets.'

Bond: 'Mouton Rothschild *is* a claret.'

They never learn, these ill-educated hoodlums, do they?

Of course, not all villains are ignorant about wine. Take my old adversary Francisco Scaramanga. He had a rather well-stocked wine cellar. When at dinner, Bond remarked on the wine, 'Excellent – slightly reminiscent of a '34 Mouton.'

Scaramanga replied, 'Then I must add it to my cellar!'

Leaving claret aside, I myself prefer a chilled bottle of Sancerre nowadays, a wine I discovered a few years ago when a group of us hired a mini-van to explore the chateaux of the Loire Valley. There, I tasted the wonderful bone-dry, highly aromatic wine with its intense flavours of peaches and gooseberries. The reason we restrict our choice largely to white wines is because, unfortunately, my wife develops terrible migraines if she consumes any red wine or a Chardonnay. Personally, I think a headache is sometimes worthwhile.

ABOVE: With Barbara Bach, or Barbara 'Back-to-Front' as I called her, in *The Spy Who Loved Me*. I'm probably thinking of two good reasons to serve champagne.

UP IN SMOKE

Bond also smokes in the novels, his preference being Morland Specials with their three gold rings, of which he consumes three or more packs a day. He tries other brands on his travels, most notably Shinsei in *You Only Live Twice*. 'He took a cigarette and lit it. It burned rapidly with something of the effect of a slow-burning firework ... it was good and sharp on the lungs with ninety per cent proof spirits. He let the smoke out in a quiet hiss and smiled.'

I didn't smoke cigarettes in my Bond films, as Sean and George had before me, and indeed as Timothy did after me. I gave up cigarettes in 1971 when, just before commencing work on *The Persuaders!*, I, along with my producing partner Bob Baker and script editor Terry Nation, visited Tony Curtis in LA. Tony was head of the anti-smoking lobby (though strangely did not include cannabis in his campaign!) and when, at his home for a meeting, we all lit up, Tony showed me a book with a rather curious photo on the front. It was a cancerous lung. It put me off

BELOW: It was Red Grant's choice of wine that gave him away as a baddie in *From Russia With Love*. Red wine with fish? Honestly!

smoking cigarettes for life, though I must admit I did still smoke cigars into the 1980s.

Contrary to popular myth, it was not part of my Bond contract that I had to be supplied with cigars. Yes, I smoked them on set, but I bought my own – much to the delight of our assistant director Derek Cracknell. Whenever he saw me light up between takes, Derek would call, 'Roger, they're ready for you!' and would offer to hold my cigar for me. Whenever I returned, saying they *weren't* ready, I'd find Derek sitting in a chair puffing away on my Davidoff.

ABOVE: In the bad old days, I smoked Davidoffs, though, contrary to popular myth, they were not supplied as part of my contract. I had to buy them.

BELOW: Sean at his Savile
Row tailors, being outfitted
for his Bond debut ... and the
finished result.

RIGHT: Sean Connery cuts
a fine figure in his Conduit
Cut suit. His elegantly attired
co-star Pedro Armendáriz was
terminally ill during filming
of *From Russia With Love*,
though kept it a secret and
completed the film in order
to provide income for his
family. He took his own life in
hospital shortly afterwards.

SARTORIAL SIMPLICITY

William Shakespeare wrote 'clothes maketh the man'. If that was
the case for the literary James Bond, then I think we'd be a little
disappointed in 'the man', to be honest. Contrary to popular
thinking, while Ian Fleming had an eye for Savile Row quality,
he rarely shopped there, preferring instead the 'off-Row' prices of
Benson, Perry and Whitley in Cork Street, just a couple of roads
along from the Row. He'd have three suits made at a time, for the
princely sum of 58 guineas each.

It was reported by Mr Whitley of said establishment that
'Mr Fleming wore his suits until they were in threads', and, 'He
dressed for comfort not for style'. This attitude clearly extended
to his hero, as in the books Bond's clothes don't vary a great deal.
His look was probably best described in Fleming's last novel, *The
Man With The Golden Gun*, where he described Jim's 'dark-blue
single-breasted suit, white shirt, thin black knitted silk tie, black
casuals' as his 'usual rig'.

In *Moonraker* Fleming had Bond wearing a 'heavy white silk shirt, dark blue trousers of navy serge, dark blue socks and well polished moccasin shoes ... put on a black knitted silk tie and his jacket ...' in readiness for an evening at Blades Club. It was sartorial simplicity.

That didn't stop him noticing other people's wardrobes, though. In the same novel Fleming wrote: 'Bond concluded his inspection with Drax's clothes, which were expensive and in excellent taste, a dark blue pinstripe in lightweight flannel, double-breasted with turn back cuffs, a heavy white silk shirt with a stiff collar, an unobtrusive tie with a small grey and white check, modest cufflinks, which looked like Cartier, and a plain gold Patek Phillippe watch with a black leather strap.'

Despite all of the descriptive detail Fleming wove into his adventures, Bond's wardrobe was by and large indistinct. No shirt maker was ever mentioned; no tailor ever credited. One thing we did garner was he liked 'single-breasted dinner jackets' and a 'heavy silk evening shirt' when it was time to enjoy the 'solid, studied comfort of card rooms and casinos', but that's about as much as Fleming ever enlightened us about his hero's tastes in attire. The films are a very different case.

BELOW: Hey, George! That's how I got into movies.

JIMBO COMES ALIVE

Bond's on-screen look is credited to Terence Young, the director of *Dr. No*. He brought in his own tailor, Anthony Sinclair of Conduit Street, and shirt maker Turnbull & Asser. Young wanted to achieve the look of a well-dressed man, but one who didn't particularly stand out from the crowd. Sean was not particularly used to wearing suits, and in order for him to feel totally at ease when filming began, Young asked that he wear suits around the clock, even to the extent of sometimes sleeping in them.

Anthony Sinclair created the classic, pared-down look of Connery's suits that came to be known as the 'Conduit Cut'. They were lightweight, one hundred per cent wool in navy blue, shades of grey and a subtle Glen Urquhart check. They were slim-line, single-breasted, two-button outfits. The Conduit Cut featured in all of Sean's early films, and changed only when Peter Hunt brought in his tailor, Dimi Major of Fulham, for *On Her Majesty's Secret Service*. Peter Hunt and his costume designer Marjory Cornelius came up with a rather timeless three-piece suit for the London scenes, featuring wider lapels and pocket flaps, and more fashionable brighter styles for the overseas settings. It was a marked departure. Bond was now outfitted from a much wider-styled wardrobe, and that gave the feeling of a slightly more casual 007 for the late sixties.

When I stepped into the role, I suggested that my long-time tailor, Cyril Castle (of Mayfair), with whom I had worked on *The Saint* and *The Persuaders!*, would give Jim a more contemporary look for the 1970s. Lots of modern colours, sports jackets and trousers became the new norm. The designs were fashionable, yet also elegant and comfortable. So much so that when Frank Sinatra and Sammy Davis Jr were in London they called to say they thought my clothes in *The Man With The Golden Gun* were very sharp – especially my dinner suits – then took themselves up to Cyril for new outfits.

After *The Spy Who Loved Me* I had, very reluctantly, left the UK due to the 87 per cent income-tax rate imposed by the then Labour government. Cubby also moved out and declared the next Bond film, *Moonraker*, would be shot in France. Initially, I based myself in Italy, at the family holiday home in Castiglione, and, in preparing for the next Bond film, realized it would be impossible

ABOVE: This was one outfit I did not try to steal after production.

for me to travel back and forward to London for wardrobe fittings. So I suggested to Cubby we could use my Italian tailor, Angelo Litricio. In the month of August it was a joy driving to Rome for fittings – the only sounds I heard on the two-hour journey were burglar alarms. Everyone was on holiday except the thieves!

Meanwhile, back in London, Douglas Hayward had fast established a reputation as a tailor to the stars – and many of my friends. Doug was a real character to say the least. His anecdotage and attitude were the source for the character Harry Pendel in John le Carré's *The Tailor of Panama*; his charming manner was the model for his friend Michael Caine's 1966 performance in *Alfie*. Doug's celebrity client roster included Peter Sellers, Terence Stamp, Richard Burton, Alan Whicker, Michael Parkinson, Rex Harrison, Jackie Stewart and Michael Caine, among many others – whom he often visited in a second-hand Mini, packed full of material. He was so passionate about serving his clients that he'd go wherever they asked. That sounded perfect to me and, apart from becoming a dear friend, he also made all my subsequent suits, right up until his untimely death in 2008.

KEEP IT SIMPLE: MAKE IT CLASSIC

The 1970s were famous for flares and wide collars, and though my Bond's look was contemporary, it was relatively restrained when you look at some of the more outrageous trends in menswear. In the early 1980s a more traditional style was introduced, with classic three-piece suits and blazers, coupled with casual coolness. I've been told – sometimes sneeringly – that nobody can carry off a safari suit quite like me.

At the time, Doug's principle was, 'Keep them as classic as possible, as I believe people will be watching Bond films in twenty years' time … keep noticeable [current fashion] details, such as turnback cuffs, to a minimum. Fred Astaire could walk down the street today in a suit that was made for him in the 1930s and look fabulous. I have always borne that in mind when making clothes for films and I don't think I have ever done work for a film I am now embarrassed by.'

One of the perks of being the so-called star of a film is that you could legitimately steal – or should I say 'request' – items of wardrobe. After all, they are tailor-made for you, so who else can use them? On *The Man With The Golden Gun* I wore a particularly nice suit for what was to be the final scene.

'Hmmm,' I thought, 'must ensure this doesn't get dirty, I'd like this one.' So I did my level best to keep the suit smart, un-creased and unblemished.

As the director called 'Cut!' I smiled widely, stroked my

BELOW: Royal Navy Commander James Bond, CMG, RNVR. Pierce was style personified in uniform.

You too could look like Bond – The Daniel Craig Bond look from *Casino Royale*

❦ Brioni supplied the formal suits and evening wear

❦ Turnbull and Asser are credited with supplying the formal shirts (handmade) and ties

❦ John Lobb supplied many of the shoes from their ready-to-wear collection

❦ La Perla made the blue 'Grigoperla' swimming trunks to costume designer Lindy Hemming's own designs

❦ Sunspel made most of the casual wear including polo shirts, pullovers, T-shirts and underwear

❦ Omega supplied two styles of wristwatch: the Planet Ocean on a black rubber strap (2900.50.91) and the Seamaster on the stainless-steel strap (2220.80)

❦ Persol made the sunglasses, model nos. 2244 & 2720

❦ Converse Jack Purcell OTR ankle boots worn during the Madagascar crane fight sequence

❦ Armani made the leather jacket.

❦ Gieves & Hawkes supplied the white braces (with gold clips) from the Casino scenes

lapels and … a huge bucket of paste came down from above and completely ruined my lovely suit, not to mention my well-groomed hair. I looked up, and saw Cubby Broccoli wetting himself with laughter. He knew I had been admiring it!

In the early 1980s the *Daily Mail* referred to me as one of Britain's best-dressed men. How kind. It's true to say I don't feel particularly comfortable in a pair of jeans and a T-shirt, and I rarely dress down when I'm out and about, except perhaps when on holiday.

If you opened my wardrobe today you'd find shirts made for me by the Swedish company Eton Shirts or perhaps a few from Frank Foster of Pall Mall. For Bond, incidentally, I had my shirts made occasionally by Turnbull and Asser but more often than not by Washington Tremlett. There's also a variety of blazers – as my weight is sometimes a little erratic I have blazers of many sizes – some made to measure and a few 'off the peg'. My shoes are always handmade by Ferragamo.

In fact, I introduced Ferragamo to the Bond films. A neighbour of mine in Italy was married to Salvatore Ferragamo's eldest son, and I took her to a premiere of *Live And Let Die*, where she was horrified to see I was wearing Gucci shoes and belt. From then on Ferragamo supplied shoes, belts and luggage for the films.

BELOW: The Other Fellas and their tuxedos. Latterly, Tom Ford has designed Daniel Craig's. When asked recently whether he still enjoyed taking home some of the costumes, Daniel said, 'When I first did Bond, I was given all these amazing suits and suddenly I've got this huge wardrobe and I'm thinking, "Oh my God, what am I going to wear?" I've kind of flipped the other way now and if I could just wear jeans and T-shirts all the time I would.'

RIGHT: Here I am after my morning swim. Or is it Daniel Craig? We look so alike it's difficult to tell.

BELOW: I'm not sure if blue towelling is still all the rage ... Shirley Eaton and Sean looking 'cool' on set.

After I hung up Jimmy's tuxedo, Timothy Dalton took over, and his interpretation of Bond went back to the books with a more edgy, tougher style. His clothes were largely his own choice from ready-to-wear shops and, as a result, were much more casual and loose-fitting than ever before. Timothy went as far as to say he felt 'more comfortable' wearing the off-the-peg range than any of the designer suits supplied.

Some say he looked a little 'too ordinary' for Her Majesty's Secret Service, with not enough occasions for black tie and more formal outfits. But maybe they miss the point of being a spy in that he should blend into the background and the times.

'I cut the wardrobe down by three-quarters. Bond was never flash or ostentatious. In fact, he really wore a uniform, a dark suit, navy blue. He was very navy blue. He wasn't a wealthy man. He used his money to buy the best that he needed, but then he kept it,' said Timothy in a 1989 interview in *Rolling Stone* magazine.

For his second film, *Licence To Kill*, costume designer Jodie Tillen, who came fresh from the TV series *Miami Vice*, suggested a few ideas, much to the chagrin of her new 007. 'She wanted to put me in pastels,' said Dalton in an interview with Garth Pearce. 'Can you imagine? I thought, "No, we can't have that." The clothes say so much about Bond. He's got a naval background, so he needs a strong, simple colour like dark blue.'

After Timothy's departure, Brioni, an Italian fashion house founded in 1945, was invited to dress the next 007 – in the shape of Pierce Brosnan. With the ability to produce many copies of the same suit, and quickly, to ensure there are numerous intact ones available for action scenes, stunt doubles and so forth, Brioni offered to donate fifty suits for *GoldenEye*. Free of charge, I might add. You see, James Bond must look impeccable at all times. He isn't allowed to get dirty, to sweat or tear his clothes. I remember being on location in India for *Octopussy*. I must have changed my shirt a dozen times one morning as, despite the heat, Jimmy could not have patches of perspiration on his outfit.

The association with Brioni continued into Daniel Craig's first outing as 007, with them making his tuxedo (said to be worth £6,000 alone). However for *Quantum of Solace* designer Tom Ford took over tailoring duties. Daniel was reported to have ruined around forty bespoke suits during filming. 'It really is a crime. It makes me weep every time. They're great suits,' he told the British press.

I just hope he managed to save a few for himself.

BOND
ON
LOCATION

BOND ON LOCATION

PREVIOUS PAGES: At the Berlin Wall in 1983 at the height of the Cold War.

LEFT: Me being brave on the Eiffel Tower. It's a long walk up there, you know, with 347 steps to the first level alone.

BELOW: On location in Jamaica, Sean thought it was time for a beer and a nap. He obviously couldn't get to sleep, and sent for more beer.

I t might actually be easier to say where Bond *hasn't* been in the world, though looking at the films, I have so far spotted him travelling to Jamaica, Croatia, Serbia, the UK, the USA, Turkey, Italy, Switzerland, France, Germany, Mexico, Japan, Portugal, Egypt, Lebanon, the Caribbean, Hong Kong, China, Austria, Brazil, Greece, Spain, Russia, Gibraltar, Morocco, Pakistan, Azerbaijan, Monaco, Cuba, South Korea, North Korea, Uganda, Montenegro, Haiti, Bolivia and Madagascar.

HOME OR AWAY?

Of course, the filmmakers didn't actually, or necessarily, visit every country – local locations were often dressed to look like somewhere else. For example, RAF Northolt, the Royal Air Force base near Pinewood Studios, doubled as a Cuban airbase in *Octopussy*, for Blue Grass Kentucky in *Goldfinger* and as an Azerbaijani airbase in *The World Is Not Enough*. The opening scenes of *Casino Royale* were filmed in the same place Sean Connery drove his Aston Martin DB5 in *Goldfinger* – Black Park, near Slough. Then there was Brent Cross shopping centre doubling for a Hamburg hotel car park in *Tomorrow Never Dies*; the Nene Valley Railway in Peterborough doubled for East Germany in *Octopussy* and again in *GoldenEye* for Russia. Amberley Working Museum in West Sussex doubled for Silicon Valley; and the IBM Building in

Staines doubled for the German HQ of Elliot Carver in *Tomorrow Never Dies*.

Typically, when planning 007's travels, a script outline comes together first, then the writer, director and producers explore potential locations in which to set the action, and from there thrash out the story some more. Many stops along the way turn out to be false trails, with nothing visually exciting to offer; others are too difficult to reach, or don't have any local infrastructure; and some are politically dodgy, so they're all ruled out. But once a likely location is confirmed, the whole team of production managers, location managers, production designer and director of photography ship out to lend their thoughts and ideas.

Then there is the important question, 'Where can we find a top-class hotel for our beloved star, whom we want to treat royally?'

In the 1960s, there were no such things as economy airlines, cheap all-inclusive package holidays – or even colour television in many homes. The only way people were able to see exotic locations and fancy hotels was by buying a ticket to see a Bond film at the cinema. Nowadays it's harder to find somewhere with which viewers aren't familiar, which is why places like Azerbaijan and Bolivia pop up on the list.

ABOVE: The height of Bondmania was marked with *Thunderball*. Here Sean arrives for filming in the Bahamas (where he now resides) with Cubby, Terence Young and Kevin McClory.

BELOW: The Peninsula Hotel, Hong Kong, with its trademark green Rolls-Royce cars. Surrounded by press when we filmed there, Britt Ekland smiled at me and said, 'Oh I do like being a film star.'

Moving around between countries with a 200+ crew is like a military exercise. Typically, in my day, we started off on location, with the unit going ahead by charter and us swanky stars – who secured a first-class flight from the kindly producers – going in a day or two later. Then, with those location scenes in the can, it was back to the studio for a few weeks before jetting off to location number two, thereby allowing the studio stages to be re-dressed with new sets to await our second coming. One therefore had to be prepared to live out of a suitcase for four or five months. Thankfully, I have a big suitcase.

BOND ON LOCATION

DOUBLING UP

I can't really go into any great detail on the locations used in the films outside of my seven, as I wasn't there. So let me tell you about me and mine ...

When Live And Let Die was in the planning stage, writer Tom Mankiewicz suggested to Guy Hamilton that they might go to New Orleans. Why? Well, because Guy liked jazz and old Jimbo hadn't been there before. It sounded like a good enough reason for a trip out there at least – not only was there jazz in New Orleans, there were bayous too.

'Wouldn't that give us a great opportunity for a boat chase?'

'Hey and there's this crocodile farm upriver ...'

'How about putting Bond in there on an island surrounded by crocs?'

'Look, there's this low bridge here. How about we put Bond in a vehicle, and have the villain *chase* him here?'

'Yes! How about a double-decker bus?'

... And that's how scripts and set pieces evolve on a Bond film, and in particular this one.

Locations featured include New Orleans, New York, Jamaica (which, of course, was also the setting for *Dr. No*) and Louisiana.

One hotel we used in Jamaica was the Couples Sans Souci,

ABOVE: The majority of *Goldfinger* was set in the USA, including this sequence featuring Honor Blackman and Sean Connery at the villain's Kentucky ranch – though it was all filmed at Pinewood. Sean did not once step foot in America!

in Ocho Rios. It doubled as Bond's San Monique base, and had, incidentally, been used as Miss Taro's home in *Dr. No* a decade earlier. Meanwhile, over at the Half Moon Bay Club in Montego Bay, bungalow 9 was used as Bond's own. The club also featured in *Casino Royale* with Daniel Craig, though it had been extensively remodelled by then – and hopefully without any unwelcome snakes slipping in.

The Man With The Golden Gun was originally planned to shoot in Iran, where part of Fleming's book was set, but the Yom Kippur War broke out. Scouts were sent to Beirut in the Lebanon instead, but declared it 'not particularly interesting' – in the filmic sense, of course. Focus quickly switched to Southeast Asia: Phang Gna Bay, Thailand; Bangkok; Macau; and Hong Kong, where the part-submerged wreck of the RMS

Queen Elizabeth was also used, and written in as a top-secret MI6 base grounded in Victoria Harbour.

From tracking down gunsmith Lazar in Macau, the former Portuguese enclave west of Hong Kong, we visited and filmed on the Floating Macau Palace – a converted vessel moored on the western shore – then took the ferry across the bay to Kowloon (the mainland suburb of Hong Kong), and the Peninsula Hotel, which famously (so Bond was told) runs a fleet of green Rolls-Royce limousines. I thought it seemed more famous for its array of shoes, until I learned Imelda Marcos was in residence.

BOTTOMS UP ...

The Bottoms Up Club, was also found in Kowloon amid the neon dazzle of the Tsim Sha Tsui shopping district. Villain Hai Fat's estate was located at the Dragon Garden on Castle Peak Road, Castle Peak. Once I'd seen him off it was on to Bangkok for a few weeks, and a boat chase through the filthy klongs that criss-cross the city.

'Under no circumstances should a drop of the water touch your lips,' we were all warned. The diseases contained therein were deemed enough to give any chemist nightmares.

Unfortunately, after taking a corner – near an undertaker's – a little too tightly in the boat (a long-tailed sampan) I was driving, I lost my balance and tipped over into the water. I stayed tight-lipped under the water to avoid the rotor blade that was whizzing about overhead, but made the mistake of opening my eyes; and saw what a 'no frills' burial meant in that particular establishment.

Other locations included the karate school in Muang Boran, about twenty miles east of town in Changwat Samut Prakan, which was actually an ancient city and the world's largest outdoor museum, with scaled-down versions of the famous buildings and temples of Bangkok. Most famously, we then moved on to Scaramanga's island hideout on Khow-Ping-Kan – one of a chain of tiny jungle-covered limestone pillars in Phang Nga Bay, Phuket.

It was a remote and undiscovered paradise at the time we filmed there, without even the most basic of facilities. The art department went ahead and built a small six-bedroomed prefabricated billet for myself, Christopher Lee, Guy Hamilton,

ABOVE: This rather odd-shaped mushroom rock is in Thailand, and housed Scaramanga's powerful solar device in *The Man With The Golden Gun*.

BELOW: It pays to advertise. The Bottoms Up Club as seen in my second Bond film. Wonder if I'd get a free drink there?

Maud Adams and Britt Ekland to lodge in. Each room contained a bed, a large circulating ceiling fan and a short step down into a toilet that was 2 foot 6 inches square, with a dripping tap and bucket to slosh out the hole between the footsteps. I worked out I could sit on the steps, do what came naturally, while washing and shaving at the same time. Cubby went one better and said if I could have given him a broom, he could 'shove it up [his] rear end and brush out the room at the same time'.

Today, it's overrun by tourists (and souvenir shops) who take the fifty-four-mile bus journey north from Phuket Town, and a short boat trip out to see 'James Bond Island', as it's now known.

ABOVE: Whilst doing a recce, the crew discovered this terrific crocodile farm entrance and wrote it into the script.

RIGHT: This innocent-looking cave doubled for Scaramanga's lair. I bravely entered with Christopher Lee only for a mass of bats to fly out (past us). I don't think they were vampire bats, though.

GOOD AND BAD

The Spy Who Loved Me started shooting in Sardinia, which became one of my favourite locations of all time, in no small way due to our being based at the Cala di Volpe. It was one of the most luxurious hotels ever, and featured in the film as Bond and Anya's hotel. I was also scheduled time to learn to ride the wet bike (or jet ski, as they are now called) in the beautiful blue sea just outside my room, which was no hardship whatsoever.

Then we set off for Cairo, arriving on my birthday, in fact. I walked onto the location set and couldn't quite understand why there were so many huge tents in the catering area. Catering manager George Crawford walked over, smiling widely, and said it was for my birthday lunch and, what's more, he'd managed to find lobsters for us all. I looked down at these green creatures he proffered – which were still moving despite having been dead for six weeks! The birthday boy did *not* have the lobster for lunch, and lived to see another year.

From Cairo it was on to Luxor, and quite probably the worst hotel in the world. The same menu was presented to us every single night of our two-week stay. It was the only large hotel in Luxor at the time, and guests seemingly only ever stayed for one night when they came to visit the temple of Karnak. My nightly meal consisted of what looked and tasted like a camel's testicle on a bun – it was difficult to figure out which was which.

ABOVE: One of the many, rather polluted, waterways we filmed on in *The Man With The Golden Gun*. We were warned to keep our lips tightly closed if we fell in. I wish I'd kept my eyes closed too, particularly near the undertaker's.

ABOVE: Despite what you may think, the pyramids were not one of Ken Adam's designs! Though they did make a wonderful backdrop for my first encounter with Jaws in *The Spy Who Loved Me*.

BELOW: Rio really is a breathtaking panorama.

I was so pleased when director Lewis Gilbert suggested we take an early plane out on our day of departure, meaning we could have a four-hour stopover in Cairo, before flying back to London. Cubby liked the sound of that. 'We can go to Shepheard's Hotel for a slap-up lunch,' he beamed.

At Cairo airport the customs officials – not realizing how undernourished we were – said we had to remain airside, as we were 'in transit' and could not therefore go into the city. But they told us not to worry, they'd prepared a couple of rooms for us to rest in. I said I'd share with Cubby while Lewis had his own room next door. No sooner had we walked in than Cubby proceeded to take his trousers off.

'I've got the part, Lewis!' I shouted through the wall.

GIDDY HEIGHTS ...

Moonraker decamped from our usual Pinewood base to Paris. Filming with the wonderfully civilized French working hours – long lunches and beautiful architecture – was only slightly frustrated by being split across three separate studios in the city.

It was then on to Venice and the delightful Hotel Danieli (although I prefer the Gritti Palace, personally) for the action sequences, spread between the city's 118 islands. The Venetian glass museum, in which Jimmy and Chang fought it out, was actually shot at Boulogne Studios – in a building that had once been a World War II Luftwaffe factory during the occupation. The sequence still holds the record for the largest amount of breakaway sugar glass used in a single scene.

After spending a family Christmas in Paris, the cast and crew travelled to Rio de Janeiro on Concorde. Unfortunately, I suffered an attack of kidney stones and had to spend a few days in a Parisian hospital before flying down to Rio, where I was immediately whisked off the plane to hair and make-up, before re-boarding to film the sequence of 007 arriving.

It was there one of the most challenging stunts ever took place, atop two cable cars on Table Mountain, two-thousand feet

ABOVE: The famous St Mark's Square in Venice with some old English actor looking lost.

BELOW: And I recommend viewing it by cable car, if there are no steel-toothed hoodlums around.

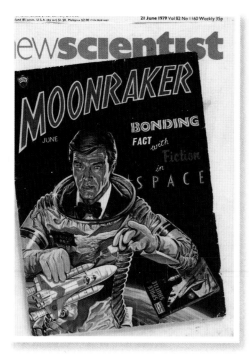

21 June 1979 Vol 82 No 1160 Weekly 35p

ABOVE: The first and only time I made the cover of *New Scientist*, here flagging up the fact that our next Bond location was going to be in space. I enjoyed the place, but it did lack atmosphere.

TOP RIGHT: When the monks discovered it was a James Bond film they'd given permission to film at their monastery, at Aghia Triatha, Meteora in Greece, they were rather upset and hung out their dirty habits ... along with tarpaulins and anything else they could find to spoil our shots. Thankfully, Cubby managed to smooth things over with a large donation to their charitable fund.

BOTTOM RIGHT: I told our caring director I hated heights. He suggested I take tranquilliser and just get on with climbing the mountain in Meteora to reach the monastery. So I did.

up in the air, with Dickie Graydon and Paul Weston doubling for Jaws and Jim Bond.

No visit to Rio would be complete without seeing the carnival. Scenes were recreated with some 700 extras to cut into footage previously shot by the second unit in the previous summer.

We then travelled inland to film at Iguassu Falls, the second largest waterfalls in the world – and perhaps the toughest of any location I've been on. There was no way of transporting equipment there, apart from carrying it on our backs from the bottom of the valley. The top of the falls was often cloaked by clouds, and Lewis suggested I should follow one of the bevy of Drax's girls across the top of the falls and inside to the hidden HQ. When I looked at the said girl I was rather taken aback – she was totally cross-eyed, and looked to my left as she spoke to me, with her eyes drifting ever further sideward. I had to follow this girl across the top of a sheer drop! I raised my concerns with Lewis that she couldn't even see straight. 'That's OK, dear,' he said. 'We'll tie a rope to your feet.'

The scene culminated in a speedboat plummeting over the top of the falls, but, due to the weather and spray, several attempts failed, so the scene was eventually shot with miniatures at the studio.

Of course it was one film where Jim also left terra firma and headed into space. The hotels there were awful. If I were you I wouldn't bother.

AND *NOT* SO GIDDY ...

From the wondrous scenes of Rio and Venice, the opening sequences of *For Your Eyes Only* took us to Stoke Poges cemetery near Slough and Becton gas works. Very glamorous! The Becton site had previously doubled for Vietnam in Stanley Kubrick's *Full Metal Jacket*, but now my brave stunt double Martin Grace held onto the outside of a helicopter, not trying to evade any military action, but rather that of a crazed bald man with a penchant for white cats.

Fortunately, we then moved on to Corfu, Cortina d'Ampezzo – the latter to film snow scenes, but ended up having to truck the white stuff in after it failed to materialize naturally – and Greece,

which was slightly more exotic than Becton, though none the less problematic.

The mountaintop monastery at Meteora, two kilometres north of Kalambaka in central Greece, was to be the scene of the film's finalé. Like twenty-three other monastries in the area, Aghia Triatha was built in a pretty inaccessible location during the Serbian–Byzantine wars of the fourteenth century, where the only access was by removable wooden ladder.

A deal was done in advance with the monks to allow us to film, though I'm not quite sure our man told them it was going to be a Bond film, as once they realized such a womanizing, gambling and ruthless character was due they protested by hanging out their washing and huge tarpaulin sheets all over the roofs. It was not the panoramic scene our cameraman had envisaged.

I tried to reason with them, saying I'd once been a saint, but that didn't go down too well. Cubby intervened and made a charitable donation, which seemed to placate their worries more readily.

The monastery can be visited today by tourists with a good head for heights, and suitably restrained clothing – but don't worry, it can be hired when you get there. Those enterprising monks think of everything.

ABOVE: The Monsoon Palace, HQ of the evil Kamal Khan. There seem to be more aerials on the roof than anything else these days, maybe all tuned into one of my old TV series?

RIGHT: Octopussy made her lair at the Lake Palace Hotel. The crew were warned not to let a drop of river water touch their lips. Many fell in, all survived.

Cortina was another interesting location we moved on to, chosen primarily for the abundance of snow. The only thing was, there wasn't any when we turned up! However, we had a wonderful stay, and filmed at the Miramonti Majestic Hotel. I remember Jim's room was number 300. It doesn't actually exist, though the balcony he is seen on does and belongs to room 108.

IF YOU KNEW CUBA ...

Octopussy was a lovely shoot. We started on 10 August 1982 at Checkpoint Charlie in West Berlin. The Berlin Wall was still in place and the Cold War had yet to defrost. In the scene, Bond and M are in a car heading to the border, and while M gets out Bond continues across to East Berlin. Of course, we couldn't do it for real and so the car drove a few yards into no man's land before John Glen called, 'Cut!' Happily, the curious East German guards didn't have time to react, as we turned around and drove back quickly.

After six days in Berlin, it was back to Pinewood Studios and UK locations, including Wansford in Cambridgeshire, for the Nene Valley Railway and the majority of the train sequences where Bond infiltrates and faces off against Orlov. The same location doubled for Russia twelve years later, when director Martin Campbell filmed the train-vs-tank sequence in *GoldenEye* along stretches of the six-mile private track.

RAF Upper Heyford, Oxfordshire, doubled for a West German Air Base where a huge circus was staged and, as mentioned earlier, RAF Northolt then doubled for Cuba, with the addition of a few carefully placed palm trees.

We then moved to India, and in particular Udaipur, the city of sunsets. There, the Lake Palace Hotel, which is spread across a four-acre island and constructed from marble on Lake Pichola, became Octopussy's floating palace. The interiors and courtyards of the palace were shot back at Pinewood, much to the relief of cast and crew, who were struggling in the high temperatures; in fact I needed a new shirt and suit jacket almost every take. As you know, of course, James Bond does not sweat, and the wardrobe and make-up department constantly touched me up in order to keep Jim looking cool and collected – no mean feat when temperatures ranged from 48 to 65 degrees Celsius.

At the nearby Shiv Niwas Palace, a team of models were flown from England to partake in the obligatory poolside shoot and when the call went out to recruit some locals for extra work, we were inundated with thousands

ABOVE: I posed outside the Brandenburg Gate with a Walther PPK in *Octopussy*. An understated presence, as always.

BELOW: Not quite California – Amberley Working Museum in West Sussex doubled for the mine where Zorin was going to trigger his dastardly plan of dominating Silicon Valley.

of people. Many had to be paid off just to leave, as we couldn't have shot; in fact it became a daily occurrence for hundreds of onlookers to appear on set. The logistics of organizing crowd control during the stunt and chase sequences proved a bit of a challenge, and not always a successful one: the bicycle rider who broke up the tuk-tuk fight was not intended to be in shot at all, he was merely passing through.

The final Indian location was the Monsoon Palace, a striking building on the hillside of Udaipur, which became the lair of evil Kamal Khan.

Oh! And while we were on location, the first English-language film ever to screen at Udaipur's largest cinema was *Moonraker*. They had good taste, I thought.

RIGHT AND BELOW: Checking the handbrake is on. The Nene Valley Railway stood in for East Germany in an exciting train sequence in *Octopussy*. It also doubled for Russia in *GoldenEye*!

NENE VALLEY RAILWAY
WELCOME TO
FERRY MEADOWS STATION

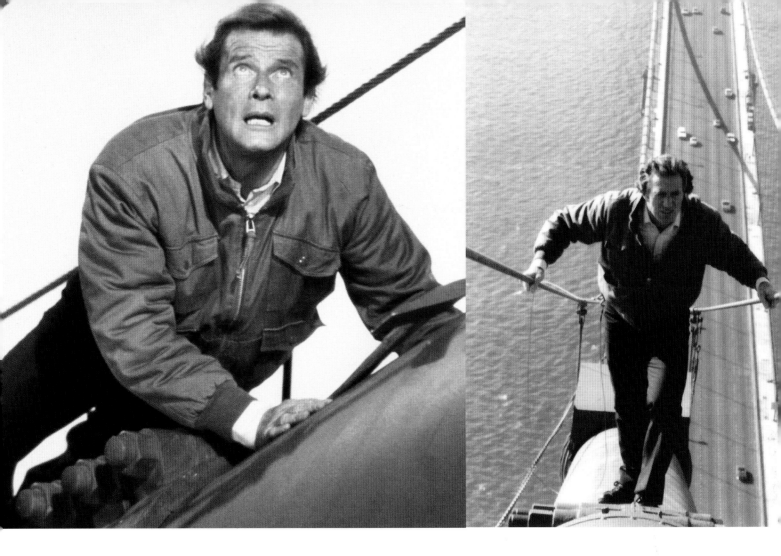

A MAYORAL FAVOURITE

A View To A Kill thankfully avoided the heat of India and Thailand and instead took us to Paris, Chantilly and, of course, San Francisco. At the end of the working day, we had somewhere to go and eat in comfortable surroundings and didn't have to worry about what we were eating!

The snowy opening in Iceland was filmed by the second unit, and I was cut in with pick-up shots at Pinewood before we all headed to Royal Ascot, and then on to Staines for the scene in which Bond and Stacey enter the Zorin mineshaft, along with the Amberley Chalk Pits Museum in West Sussex, which both doubled for California.

When San Francisco was touted as a filming location, Cubby sought the necessary permissions from the Mayor's office – the Mayor at that time being Diane Feinstein – explaining they'd like to set City Hall on fire, stage a chase with a fire engine through the streets, and film the climax on top of the Golden

ABOVE RIGHT: We filmed the climax to *A View To A Kill* on the Golden Gate Bridge. Here my brave stunt double Martin Grace climbs up to the top, some 227 metres above the water.

ABOVE LEFT: Whereas I filmed my close-ups on a Pinewood set out on the backlot, just a few metres above the ground.

ABOVE: City Hall, San Francisco. Our special-effects team carefully laid smoke pots and started controlled fires on parts of the exterior. I believe we were one of the few film crews, if not the only one, ever allowed to wreak such havoc with the full blessing of the Mayor.

Gate Bridge. The response was not particularly positive.

'Who is playing Bond?' Mayor Feinstein asked.

'Roger Moore.'

'Roger Moore? Ah! I like him,' she replied. 'What can I do to help, Mr Broccoli?'

The only caveat to our filming atop the bridge was that there couldn't be any fighting – there could be a bit of a struggle, but no out-and-out fight. My brave stunt double Martin Grace climbed to the top of the bridge – after earlier holding onto the guy rope of the airship as it crossed the harbour – to perform the final tussle, while part of the bridge was then reconstructed on the Pinewood backlot for me to film my close-ups, looking very brave.

There were even mightier heights to climb, as in Paris it was planned that B.J. Worth would film a parachute jump off the Eiffel Tower, after I had chased Grace Jones up most of it. Curiously, while permission had been granted for the jump, as the landing was going to be on a boat cruising down the Seine, that came under a different authority, and at first they refused permission: we could jump, but couldn't land. However, eventually all was smoothed over ...

PINEWOOD BOUND

Of course, I must also pay homage to the home of 007 and indeed my second home, Pinewood Studios. I shot all of my films – except *Moonraker* – out of Pinewood, and have a huge affection and appreciation for the studio. For many years my office was right next door to Cubby's, and I'd like to think we were good neighbours. Now Barbara and Michael occupy Cubby's office and the tradition continues. The studio has featured extensively in the films – Goldfinger's factory was the studio 'covered way' on the lot; the opening shots in *From Russia With Love* were filmed in the gardens; in *The World Is Not Enough* villainous Reynard hid away in the Pinewood pond grotto; the Ice Palace exterior in *Die Another Day* was all built on the backlot; and, of course, the huge volcano set in *You Only Live Twice* stood next to the present site of the 007 stage and could be seen from miles away. Pinewood and Bond are linked very closely, and hopefully will be for many years to come.

Of course, since my time Jimmy has ventured to all manner of new interesting places outside the studio walls; in particular, behind the Iron Curtain and Eastern Blocks. Where will he go next we ask? Well, *Skyfall* was rumoured to be returning to India, but then switched to Turkey instead, where the action sequences could be better accommodated. There were also rumours abound about South Africa and China.

One thing is for sure: when the phone rings next and a voice says, 'I'm working for Eon Productions and would like to talk about shooting the next Bond film in your country ...' they'll be greeted with open arms.

BELOW: On location in Chantilly – it may just be two of us in shot, but a lot goes on behind the camera!

BOND
ON
BONDS

BOND ON BONDS

PREVIOUS PAGE: George Lazenby, Timothy Dalton and me at the BAFTA fortieth anniversary tribute. I guess that makes us 00-21.

BELOW: Harry, Sean, Diane Cilento and Cubby photographed just after Sean signed his multi-picture Bond contract in London.

OPPOSITE TOP: A very youthful looking Sean in one of his first publicity shots for *Dr. No*.

OPPOSITE BOTTOM: Twenty-one years after *Dr. No*, Sean returned in *Never Say Never Again*; a title coined by his wife Micheline after he famously quit the role in 1971, vowing never again.

'm often asked, 'Who is the best Bond?'

'Apart from myself?' I modestly enquire. 'It has to be Sean.'

Sean *was* Bond. He created Bond. He embodied Bond and because of Sean, Bond became an instantly recognizable character the world over – he was rough, tough, mean and witty. Of course, it was an alter ego he didn't always appreciate, but it was one I'd like to think he is ultimately proud of – as he was a bloody good 007.

I first met Sean in the early 1960s at Arlington House in London, at a reception hosted by actress Binnie Barnes and her husband, film producer Mike Frankovich. Sean was there with his then wife Diane Cilento. Apart from his imposing size, the things I remember most from that first meeting were his amazing eyes. I'm happy to say that our meeting at that party

marked the start of a friendship that goes on to this day.

It's no secret that, after *Thunderball*, Sean was becoming disenchanted with the films. He'd helped establish the character internationally and everywhere he went there was merchandise with his image on it. However, he wasn't receiving any extra remuneration and what with that, the constant media attention and the pressure of being Bond causing a rift in his marriage, he obviously felt that no one part was worth all this.

Terence Young told the producers, 'Take Sean as a partner, make it Cubby, Harry and Sean. Sean will stay with you because he's a Scotsman. He likes the sound of gold coins clinking together. He likes the lovely soft rustle of paper. He'll stay with you if he's a partner, but not if you use him as a hired employee.'

Cubby and Harry didn't want another partner at Eon, and so Sean announced *You Only Live Twice* would be his last appearance as 007. At the Royal Charity premiere, even Her Majesty the Queen asked him, 'Is this really your last James Bond film?'

'I'm afraid so, Ma'am,' he told her.

Though Harry and Cubby reportedly offered Sean just under a million dollars to appear in *On Her Majesty's Secret Service*, he turned it down.

Thinking he might take advantage of Sean's disenchantment after *Thunderball* premiered, Charles Feldman, who had acquired the film rights to *Casino Royale*, tried to interest Sean in starring in his movie. Feldman had intended it as a thriller but when Sean declined Feldman abandoned the idea and turned it into a comedy instead. With seven directors and numerous writers, it ended up a confusing mess and a box office disaster, despite featuring David Niven as Sir James Bond and an incredible cast including Ursula Andress, Peter Sellers, Woody Allen, Orson Welles, Deborah Kerr, William Holden and John Huston.

On Her Majesty's Secret Service did respectable business at the box office without Sean, but George Lazenby made it clear that it was his one and only appearance as 007. United Artists were desperate to keep their cash cow on track, and David Picker – president of United Artists – met with Sean to agree a return for *Diamonds Are Forever*. American actor John Gavin had been in the frame and was offered a multi-picture contract, but a week before filming started Sean agreed to take on the role once more and Gavin was paid off.

Sean had been made an offer he simply couldn't refuse: David Picker had guaranteed him $1¾ million, plus a percentage of the profits, and agreed to provide financial backing for two films of Sean's choice.

Sean was then reputedly offered $5 million to return to Bond in *Live And Let Die*, but refused saying, 'Never again'. I'm very grateful to him – and, of course, work cheaper too.

SEAN CONNERY IS JAMES BOND IN NEVER SAY NEVER AGAIN

JACK SCHWARTZMAN & KEVIN McCLORY PRESENT A TALIAFILM
HAIR BY CROWN TOPPER. FACIAL WORK BY CEMENTATION, CORSETS BY JANET REGER. PG

"They say the wheelchair chase is fantastic."

R THE FIRST TIME... A HEAD-ON FILM CLASH
BATTLE OF THE B

ABOVE: The press like to stir things up, and the 'Battle of the Bonds' was good headline material; that and poking fun at our advancing ages.

NEVER SAY WHAT?

But another story was forming in the wings. With his ten-year restriction over, Kevin McClory began to make plans to rework the *Thunderball* plot for the screen again.

He engaged Len Deighton as his co-writer on the project, *James Bond Of The Secret Service*, and secured backing from Paramount Pictures. Then, in what was to prove a masterstroke, he approached Sean to become involved in the screenplay. Who knew the character better than Sean?

Sean agreed and relished his new creative role.

'The three of us did a screenplay and put all sorts of exotic events in it,' he said. 'You remember the aircraft that were disappearing over the Bermuda Triangle? We had SPECTRE doing that. There was also this fantastic fleet of planes under the sea – and they were going to be used to attack the financial centre of New York by going through the city's sewers – which you can do – right into Wall Street.

'There were going to be mechanical sharks in the bay, a take-over of the Statue of Liberty and the main line of troops on Ellis Island. All that sort of thing.'

The title changed to *Warhead*.

There was a rumour Sean would play Bond, with Orson Welles

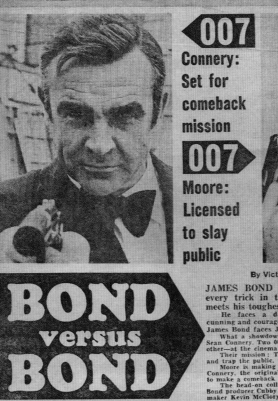

007
Connery:
Set for
comeback
mission

007
Moore:
Licensed
to slay
public

BOND versus BOND

By Victor Davis

JAMES BOND will have to use every trick in the book when he meets his toughest opponent yet.

He faces a daredevil whose skill, cunning and courage match his own. For James Bond faces James Bond.

What a showdown. Roger Moore against Sean Connery. Two 007s licensed to kill each other—at the cinema box office.

Their mission : To pull out all the stops and trap the public.

Moore is making his fourth Bond movie. Connery, the original 007, is almost certain to make a comeback in the role.

The head-on collision is because veteran Bond producer Cubby Broccoli and Irish film-maker Kevin McClory, now both possess film rights to the late Ian Fleming's stories.

Paramount Pictures announced last night that they are backing McClory to make " James Bond of the Secret Service," next spring.

Rich

The screenplay is the joint work of McClory, Connery and best-selling novelist Len Deighton. Connery looks set for the part.

Broccoli's next Bond movie is " Moonraker," starring Roger Moore. It

Producers spy a box-office bonanza

Producer Broccoli

goes into production in Paris next month.

The Bond pickings are rich. The Broccoli series—10 so far—are backed by United Artists and have earned more than £200 million at the box office.

McClory was involved in the 1965 production of "Thunderball," starring Connery.

But he then agreed to a 10-year legal freeze on making any more 007 movies.

as a villain and Trevor Howard as M, but the Fleming Estate sued and Paramount pulled out of the venture.

The flurry of news as reported in the trade journals brought the fact that Sean was now involved to the attention of Jack Schwartzman, executive vice president of Lorimer and husband of Talia Shire – with whom I made a film called *Bed And Breakfast*.

He raised the money required from twenty-five independent backers and restricted the plot back to that of *Thunderball*, thus avoiding any further legal complications.

Once Sean had written the script, he started to care about the character he'd previously tired of. By this time, Sean had divorced Diane and married his second wife Micheline, who, having heard the rumours of his return as Bond, asked that if he was enjoying it so much, why not play the part again? Adding he should never say never again … which, of course, became the title.

There were various legal issues still to be resolved, not least Cubby Broccoli's lawsuit over the filmic ownership of 007, which was eventually agreed out of court and which gave Cubby a percentage of the *Never Say Never Again* box office.

Sean's film swung into production at Elstree Studios around about the same time as I started shooting *Octopussy* at Pinewood. The press made a splash about our going head to head, with both aiming for a summer 1983 release. *Never Say Never Again* in fact opted for a Christmas release so as not to split the summer audience.

I met Sean occasionally for dinner in London during shooting, and still do to this day. He's a very talented actor, and outside of Bond has turned in some fun, impressive and lucrative performances. It's a shame we never got to do one together.

THE OTHER FELLA

When Cubby and Harry told me they'd signed an unknown model and former car salesman to play Bond, I was intrigued.

George Lazenby was incredibly laid back, and the first time I met him – at a cocktail party hosted by Cubby – he greeted me with, 'You all right, mate?'

I've met him several times over the years since, and he's always been equally pleasant and chatty. Though the last time we met in New York a few years ago he was somewhat more subdued, coming to terms with impending divorce and the effect that might have on his relationship with his young children.

I thought his was a great film, with style, energy and a terrific story, though I also felt it was helped along greatly by George Baker's dubbing of the character in a third of the film; something Lazenby wasn't aware of until he went to the premiere.

Of course, Lazenby had announced he was only going to make one movie, on the advice of his friend Ronan O'Rahilly, a music promoter who owned Radio Caroline, the famous pirate radio ship.

'He was introducing me to the Beatles and people like that, y'know …' George said. 'He took me to see them and said, "You know, Bond is over, it's finished." The movie that was out at the time was *Easy Rider*. And, you know, you had to look like one of those guys, a hippie. And so I believed him and he said, "You know, Clint Eastwood's over there doing spaghetti westerns, getting a million bucks a go. You can do those things and make a couple of them in a couple of months and you got the million dollars. Don't worry about the money." I listened to that.'

On Her Majesty's Secret Service director Peter Hunt made a conscious decision not to explain the change from Sean to George in the role of Jimmy Bond; it was just something audiences would (hopefully) accept. And in Maurice Binder's opening credits, scenes from earlier Bond films were incorporated to underline the fact it was the same series. The one nod George gave to Sean was when he delivered the line, 'This never happened to the other fella'.

It actually came about because George, doing his own stunts, said jokingly to the crew, 'The other fella never had to do this!'

Peter Hunt overheard the remark and said, 'Say that line after the opening scene.' So he did.

Fatally, for United Artists, Lazenby never signed a contract. His adviser, O'Rahilly, sent the contract to his lawyer, 'who was a real-estate lawyer', and he kept sending it back. This went on throughout the filming of *On her Majesty's Secret Service*. United Artists, meanwhile, thought he'd signed for seven movies.

George told me he was paid a $50,000 flat fee for the movie. They offered him $1 million to come back for a second, but he refused.

I know after Timothy Dalton had bowed out, George made a call to Cubby saying he was available. It was said half-jokingly, but given the chance I'm sure George would have turned in a good performance. The role went to Pierce, of course, and when we were leaving the *Die Another Day* premiere, I heard someone ask George what he thought of it and Pierce. 'It's made for young folk. It's loud, full of action and doesn't give you a rest. It's one bang after another!'

BELOW: George Lazenby at the Dorchester Hotel in London, having been unveiled as the new 007.

ROUGHER, TOUGHER

Cubby had thought of Timothy as a potential 007 a couple of decades earlier but Timothy, probably very wisely, felt he was too young to play the character: 'There was a time when Sean Connery gave up the role. I guess I, alongside quite a few other actors, was approached about the possibility of playing the part,' he said. 'That was for *On Her Majesty's Secret Service*. I was very flattered, but I think anybody would have been off their head to have taken over from Connery. I was also too young, Bond should be a man in his mid-thirties, at least – a mature adult who has been around.'

When I retired from the role in late 1985, Timothy was approached but was then committed to a London theatre production and a film, *Brenda Starr*, with Brooke Shields.

And so Cubby settled on the thirty-three-year-old Pierce Brosnan. As luck had it, with audience figures in decline, NBC had

"THANKS, SIMON, NOW WOULD YOUR GRANDAD SIGN, PLEASE?"

just cancelled Pierce's TV show *Remington Steele*, but as word broke of Eon's interest, NBC suddenly decided to renew the show and exercise their option on Brosnan's contract.

Pierce had no choice but to press on with what was to be the final series of the show. Cubby tried to strike a deal whereby Brosnan could have made a couple of feature-length episodes either side of a Bond film, but NBC and production outfit MTM declined and offered up their own alternative terms – from which Cubby walked away.

Pierce was devastated and Cubby had a production looming without a star attached.

Sam Neill was briefly considered, as was an unknown Australian actor, Finlay Light, but Cubby went back to his first choice, Timothy Dalton, again and told him he was prepared to wait the six weeks until Timothy became available.

On 6 August 1986, Eon Productions announced they had signed their new Bond – Welshman Timothy Dalton. He won both

OPPOSITE TOP: Timothy Dalton was a tougher and younger Bond.

OPPOSITE BOTTOM AND BELOW: Lucky I have a sense of humour! As though I needed reminding I was in my mid-fifties, the British press kindly did so with a couple of newspaper cartoons. Ah to be fifty-six again!

"... AND HERE'S YOUR LATEST GADGET, JAMES—A TURBO-CHARGED WHEELCHAIR"

ABOVE: On location with *The Living Daylights*. Michael Wilson, Cubby, Timothy and (far right) director John Glen. Whoever said there was a lot of standing around on film sets?

my and Sean Connery's approval; we both wished Timothy well in the role.

I read there was going to be a change in style with the new Bond: he was going to be less of a womaniser, tougher and closer to the darker character Ian Fleming wrote about. They wanted to get back to 'Fleming's Bond'.

With *The Living Daylights* on release, Eon started planning the next adventure, *Licence Revoked* (the title was later changed to *Licence To Kill* after research suggested a vast number of people didn't know what 'Licence Revoked' meant). As per Timothy's desire to see a darker Bond, the mission centred on a personal vendetta: avenging the brutal attack on Bond's long-time CIA friend, Felix Leiter.

It became the first Bond film to receive a 15 rating in the UK because of 'the level of on-screen violence and realism'.

The film opened in the summer of 1989 and found itself going head to head with other blockbuster action movies, including *Lethal Weapon 2*, *Indiana Jones And The Last Crusade* and *Batman*.

Its lower-than-anticipated worldwide gross caused MGM/ United Artists to get nervous. Cubby began to wonder if the twenty-seven-year-old franchise needed a new captain, and put Eon's parent company, Danjaq, up for sale with an asking price of £200 million.

Timothy was quoted as saying, 'My feeling is this will be the last one. I don't mean my last one. I mean the end of the whole lot. I don't speak with any real authority, but it's sort of a feeling I have. Sorry!'

However, a major spanner was thrown in the works when MGM/United Artists was sold to the Australian-based broadcasting group Qintex, which in turn wanted to merge the company with Pathé. In doing so, the Bond back catalogue was licensed to Pathé for broadcast at sums below what was considered the commercial rate. Danjaq sued.

Eon commenced pre-production of another film in May 1990, and some details were unveiled at the Cannes Film Festival around the same time, mentioning that a detailed story draft had been written by Alfonso Ruggiero Jr and Michael G. Wilson.

However, owing to the ongoing legal disputes, the production of Timothy Dalton's third film was postponed several times. In an interview in 1993, Timothy said Michael France was writing the story for the film, which was 'due to begin production in January or February 1994'.

With continuing delays and uncertainty, Timothy's six-year contract expired in 1993 (which was originally scheduled to be the year of his fourth film), and after he read Michael France's screenplay for Bond 17 he made, and subsequently announced, on

ABOVE: My dear friend David Hedison has the distinction of being the first actor to play Felix Leiter twice, first in *Live And Let Die* and, here, in *Licence To Kill* with the other fella.

12 April 1994, his decision to leave the series. It was now five years since his last outing and he felt the time had come to move on.

It had been reported in the press that the Broccolis were supposedly under pressure from MGM to replace Timothy. Whether that was true or not I don't know, but Eon respected his decision and did not to stand in his way. The search was on for his replacement.

Timothy said at the time of his resignation, 'Even though the [producers] have always made it clear to me that they want me to resume my role in their next James Bond feature, I have now made this difficult decision. As an actor, I believe it is now time to leave that wonderful image behind and accept the challenge of new ones.'

By this time, Cubby's health was suffering and my dear friend could no longer be as active in the new production as he would have liked. When I saw him for one of the last times at his home in California, he told me of his excitement at casting Pierce Brosnan, and that Michael and Barbara would be taking the helm.

Pierce was unveiled as the new 007 on 7 June 1994 in London, while sporting a full beard for an upcoming TV movie of *Robinson*

Crusoe. His first outing was to be called *GoldenEye*, after Ian Fleming's home in Jamaica, and was to be one of a three-film contract (with an option for a fourth). Pierce also separately negotiated a production deal with MGM for his own films, the most successful of which was *The Thomas Crown Affair*.

When that fourth film option was picked up, and a press launch arranged at Pinewood for *Die Another Day* in 2002, Pierce was, of course, asked if he'd be doing any more. He replied that he'd like to do one more, a fifth. Plans swung into action for a fifth film in 2004, and some suggested it might be an adaptation of Ian Fleming's *Casino Royale*. Negotiations stalled, and in July 2004 Pierce announced he was leaving Bond behind him, albeit – from what I saw of him – somewhat reluctantly.

OPPOSITE: They sent for me! It was also my turn to wear the beard we shared.

BELOW: Cool, calculated and too damn handsome!

AND BOND GOES ON

OPPOSITE: I seemed to be in the minority when I championed Daniel Craig as Bond. Nice to think we proved the doubters wrong!

BELOW: Timothy Dalton with Barbara Broccoli at the tribute to Cubby Broccoli at the Odeon Leicester Square.

The rumour mills swung into overtime on the subject of who would be the next James Bond. Names were bandied around, including Clive Owen, Hugh Jackman, Liam Neeson and Daniel Craig. I personally liked the idea of Daniel Craig, having seen him in *The Mother*, *Munich* and *Layer Cake*. He's a bloody good actor.

The day before Daniel was confirmed as 007, Barbara Broccoli emailed me to tell me of their choice. I was delighted – and it was my birthday too. However, it seemed, at first, that I was in a minority. The British press all but vilified him: too short, too blond, not good-looking enough, and they took great joy in mocking Daniel for wearing a life jacket on board the military launch that brought him speeding up the Thames to a press conference with waiting journalists.

I had never experienced such a massive hate campaign. Websites were set up demanding Pierce Brosnan be reinstated and peddling very negative comments and opinions about Daniel. I felt hugely sorry for Daniel, as, although he would have turned a blind eye to them, he would have been very aware of what was being said. Concentrating on the positive, he confirmed, 'We have got an incredible script, and that is my first line of attack. Once I read it, I knew I did not have any choice, I had to go for it. It is a huge challenge, and I think life is about challenges ... Together with Martin [Campbell, director], I want to make the best film we can, the most entertaining film we can.'

The doubters were soon silenced – and many were converted.

I didn't get to meet Daniel until 5 October 2008. We were both at the London Palladium attending the centenary celebration for Ian Fleming; in fact, we shared a dressing room. I arrived early to ensure I got the best mirror, and when Daniel arrived he grabbed me, hugged me tightly and greeted me like a long-lost friend.

His Bond is terrific, and I hope he'll reign for many years to come.

BELOW: You won't catch a bus standing there, mate. Daniel looking cool and very elegant as Jim Bond.

The only piece of advice I'd offer anyone regarding playing Jimbo is you use what you have in your own personality and be true to yourself, while stealing a bit here and there for added effect.

Nostalgia is quite handy too, as you'll find people who are rather unforgiving at the time often rediscover you in later life. Many is the time I have been stopped by someone who has thanked me for my Bond films, saying they enjoy them for their entertainment value and how well they still stand up.

In closing, my admiration goes to Barbara and Michael above anyone else, for holding this extraordinary franchise – established by Cubby and Harry – together for so many years. I can see it lasting another fifty.

BELOW: You won't catch a bus standing there, mate. Daniel looking cool and very elegant as Jim Bond.

Felix Leiter

Felix Leiter, Bond's brother from Langley, first appeared in Ian Fleming's novel *Casino Royale*. His name originates with two of Fleming's friends: 'Felix' being the middle name of Ivor Bryce, while 'Leiter' was the surname of Marion Oates Leiter Charles, then wife of Thomas Leiter.

On film, the CIA operative was initially portrayed by Jack Lord (left), of *Hawaii Five-O* fame. When the character returned in *Goldfinger*, Lord apparently demanded star billing and a much larger fee, leading to him being re-cast by Cec Linder. Two other actors took

the part, Rick Van Nutter in *Thunderball* and Norman Burton in *Diamonds Are Forever* before my great friend David Hedison (right) took the part in *Live And Let Die*. We'd worked together on *The Saint*, and I found David's easy charm, great sense of humour and professionalism to be infectious. He is such a lovely, lovely man. When ideas were passed around about casting Leiter, I suggested David. He went in to see the casting director and the rest is history. We have since worked on two more movies together, so far.

David returned in 1989 for Timothy Dalton's *Licence To Kill* as the story about Bond seeking revenge for his friend's misfortune was felt to work better if the audiences recognized Felix from an earlier adventure. He became the only actor to play the part twice; that is until Daniel Craig's films when Jeffrey Wright (bottom right) appeared in both *Casino Royale* and *Quantum of Solace* as Felix, the second African-American to be cast in the role after Bernie Casey (below) in *Never Say Never Again*. John Terry also played the part in *The Living Daylights*.

BOND
BEHIND
THE
SCENES

BOND BEHIND THE SCENES

There are a huge number of people involved in each Bond film, hundreds in fact. From the producers (who raise the money), directors (who spend it) and writers (who imagine more elaborate ways to spend it than the director could think of last time) to the assistant directors, cameramen, sound recordists, props, continuity, editors, stunt team, production managers, oh and yes, the actors. We all come together and form one big happy family for six or seven months, before going our separate ways to do other things, and await the next Bond a year or so later to bring us back together.

A FAMILY AFFAIR

With Cubby Broccoli at the helm it became very much a family atmosphere on the movies with a family team – and I think I'm correct in saying that some crew members today are from the second or even third generation to work on a 007 film. Even my sons and daughter have been involved – Geoffrey as a third assistant director on my final Bond; Christian in the location department on *GoldenEye*; and on screen, in Deborah's case, as a 'Bond girl' in *Die Another Day*. She often says to me her small role as an air stewardess still prompts more mail than anything else that hits her doormat, including bills – and you know how thick and fast they arrive.

The established production pattern during my tenure was one film pretty much every two years. They opened in the summer, generally, with a London premiere and a week or two exclusive presentation following, at the Odeon Leicester Square, before a nationwide release. The worldwide release followed with Europe, the USA, Australasia and then – finally – Japan, all involving junkets and promotional events. It could often be a good month or two from the beginning to the end of the PR trail. Needless to say, the questions at these events became a little repetitive, usually starting off with, 'Who is your favourite Bond girl?', 'Who is your favourite villain?' and 'Which is your favourite film?' – 'This one,' I'd reply without hesitation.

I often used to amuse myself by slipping in statements, such as the best thing about location work was that I could steal the hotel towels, or that I did all my own stunts apart from the sex scenes, and that sort of thing. I was often quoted verbatim. Which taught me that some people just don't share my sense of humour.

At the time of a premiere, and with the United Artists executives happy with what they had on their hands, the script for the following Bond film was commissioned and within six months Eon, the production company, would move into pre-production with it – usually for three or four months – in which time they designed sets, brought in the key crew members to scout locations, planned effects, designed and bought costumes, settled camera requirements and so on, ahead of the shoot. So, even though there were two years between films, the time between finishing one and starting another was really quite minimal. Fortunately, we actors tended to bugger off after the last day of shooting and, apart from a bit of dubbing work, didn't really turn up again until premiere time. Then there'd be a break until a few weeks before shooting commenced on the next adventure, allowing time to tackle a couple of other films in between. Make hay while the sun shines, I say.

ABOVE: Dear Barbara Broccoli ... I'd like to play a villain please, Love, Roger Moore.

BELOW: Behind-the-scenes photography.

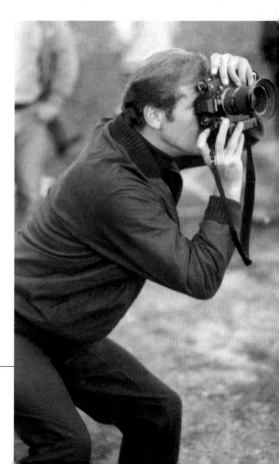

ABOVE: Dear Lewis Gilbert is one of the most gentle gentlemen in the film business, and guided me through two of my adventures.

BELOW: A typical Eon call sheet, this being for *Goldfinger*. I never bothered to keep any of mine – as they'd be on eBay if I had.

AS SEEN ON SCREEN

Of course, several of the other offered projects were very Bondian in style or character. But while there were no contractual restrictions with Eon on my doing anything else, I did feel it would be unwise to prostitute myself in Jimmy Bond rip-offs. It would only serve to damage my credibility – and I didn't want to appear ungrateful to Cubby, either. The odd car commercial in Japan (and only shown in Japan) and an appearance on *The Muppet Show* aside, the nearest I got to playing Jim in another film was in *The Cannonball Run*. In it, I suggested that while I wouldn't appear on screen as JB, I'd happily send myself up; so my character, Seymour Goldfarb Jr, believed he was a daft English actor called Roger Moore. How could I decline a lovely role like that?

Consequently, being away earning a living, I was never closely involved in the 007 scripting process – well, I can hardly act, let alone do anything else creative – though once contracts were agreed, I would have discussions with the writers, directors and producers and go through anything I felt uneasy about: sometimes they asked for one eyebrow too many to be raised, or perhaps there weren't enough love scenes. Then it was into costume fittings, a bit of PR to launch things and learning lines. Unfortunately, being the hero, you're in pretty much every scene, so there's no bunking off.

The first script on a Bond usually bears little resemblance to the final draft. The big set pieces and some important dialogue scenes are always locked, but everything else changed and evolved as we went on, and I'm sure still does to this day with Daniel Craig's adventures. Although only two or three writers are ever credited with the screenplay (due to Writers' Guild rules), there can be a significant number involved in developing story ideas, treatments and on rewrites. The first script is always typed on white pages, and any changes are then slipped in on coloured ones. Each set of changes required new coloured pages, and as there were many drafts of each change there were, accordingly, many different-coloured pages, with script spines resembling a rainbow. It was rare that a final script contained many (if any) white pages.

When I worked with director Lewis Gilbert, I would arrive on set having dutifully learned my pages and Lewis would say, 'OK, dear, what are you going to say today?'

'Well, what's in the script ...' I replied.

'Oh, I think we can improve on that ...' he'd say, in his uniquely vague manner, and put his copy down.

I don't think our screenwriter, Christopher Wood, was particularly enamoured with my playing around with his words after he had wrestled and sweated to craft them, but I hope the pay cheques eased his frustration with this foolish actor. I always made sure I delivered the lines about how the villain planned to destroy the world, and stuck to the choreographed and rehearsed action and fight scenes. The rest was fair game.

FIRST IMPRESSIONS

On seeing the film of *Dr. No* for the first time, Ian Fleming's verdict was, 'Dreadful. Simply dreadful.' In public he was a little more diplomatic and said, 'Those who have read the books will be disappointed, but those who haven't will find it a wonderful movie. Audiences laugh in all the right places.'

I never met Ian Fleming. However, when I arrived in Jamaica to make *Live And Let Die* I was invited to visit Goldeneye, Fleming's house on the north coast, where he wrote the Bond novels. It was a large sprawling bungalow, occupying a former donkey racecourse and set in fifteen acres of grounds. It was all painted white with large shuttered windows. It looked a bit like a hospital building

BELOW: Tom Mankiewicz (right, with Guy Hamilton centre) worked on three films as screenwriter, and gave me some of my very best lines. Thanks, Tom.

ABOVE: This was lunch after Harry took away the tablecloths and silverware. Guy Hamilton (in the sunglasses) doesn't look too impressed, does he?

BELOW: Dear Michael Wilson ... I'd like to play a villain please. Kind regards, Roger Moore.

from *Sanders of the River*. It still had his desk in place and various copies of his books dotted around the shelves. It was quite a humbling experience walking around and thinking, 'This is where it all started.'

Incidentally, I did share Fleming's view of *Dr. No* being a film of laughs. Cubby and Harry were perplexed when I said they had a fun picture on their hands. They thought it was a dark thriller.

Fleming saw only the first couple of Eon produced films, as sadly he died during the production of *Goldfinger* in 1964. He had witnessed only a little of the success his creation was about to achieve. Cubby Broccoli declared that Fleming's name should be on the front title of every film, even after they had exhausted his novels as titles. In my case the above-the-title legend read:

'Albert R. Broccoli presents Roger Moore as Ian Fleming's James Bond 007 in ...'

When Cubby passed away, his children Barbara and Michael declared that his name too would still appear above the title, hence you now see:

'Albert R. Broccoli's Eon Productions presents Daniel Craig as Ian Fleming's James Bond 007 in ...'

And nobody, but nobody, apart from the actor playing Jim, has their name above the title. Many have asked, but Cubby always said, 'nobody is bigger than James Bond'.

There's no arguing with that!

NOT ALWAYS HARMONIOUS

By the time I made my first Bond, the relationship between Cubby and Harry Saltzman was strained. So much so they divided their duties on each film – *Diamonds Are Forever* was largely overseen by Cubby, whereas *Live And Let Die* was, on the whole, Harry's picture, and then Cubby took the main helm of *The Man With The Golden Gun*.

Many newspaper reports had surfaced about the tensions and arguments between the two producers, and Guy Hamilton summed it up well to United Artists' executives visiting the set: 'I can work very happily with Cubby, and I can work very happily with Harry. But working with Cubby and Harry together is a nightmare.'

I liked them both greatly, but sometimes had to dodge the crossfire.

In an interview with the *Daily Mail* in 1973, Harry admitted that, with only five more Fleming stories left, he had every intention of getting out when the going was good. On 11 November that year another story, this time in the London *Evening Standard*, suggested that Harry had engaged lawyers to sell his share in Danjaq, the company he co-owned with Cubby, to Columbia Pictures.

Cubby had approval on any deal, and would have been aghast that his partner was contemplating bailing out and placing him in the hands of a distributor other than UA, who had bankrolled all the films to date.

Harry was undoubtedly in dire financial straits. Two of his more recent films – *The Battle Of Britain* and *Toomorrow* – were not the box office successes he had hoped for. Harry had invested heavily in these projects, as he had in a club in London and in buying Technicolor. He also began mounting a bid to buy Shepperton Studios. He used his collateral in Bond and Danjaq as security against bank loans – something his partnership agreement with Cubby specifically forbade. The banks started foreclosing, and Harry had no option but to sell. But to whom?

Harry started discussions with UA's Arthur Krim. A week after *The*

BELOW: Ian Fleming with his two producers – Harry and Cubby.

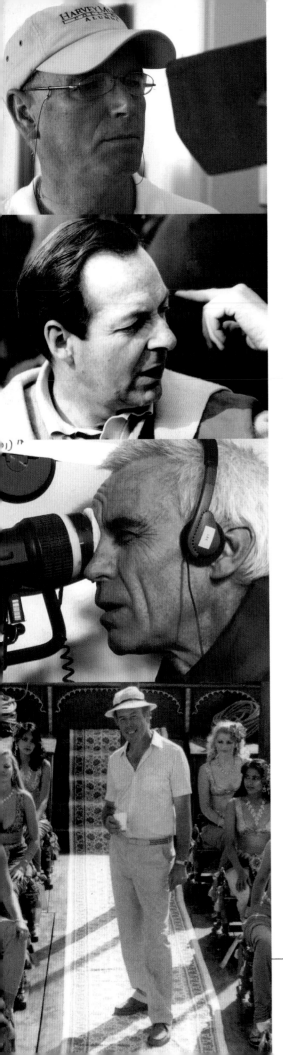

Man With The Golden Gun premiered, UA sealed a deal to buy Harry out – for a reported £20 million.

It was a deal – and a new partner – Cubby felt he could live with and he split from Harry, and not on particularly happy terms.

Jacqueline, Harry's wife, sadly succumbed to cancer when we were filming *The Spy Who Loved Me* and Harry seemed to go downhill afterwards. He sold his beloved Buckinghamshire home, moved to the States, and all but withdrew from filmmaking. He did though own a controlling share of H.M. Tennent, the West End theatre company, and eventually made just two more films, *Nijinsky* in 1980 and *Dom Za Vesanje* nine years later.

In 1981, Cubby decided to invite Harry and his family to the premiere of *For Your Eyes Only*. The hatchet was well and truly buried and Harry commented on what a great job Cubby had done with Bond.

Harry passed away in Paris in 1994.

A HOME AT PINEWOOD

I have worked with most of the talented team of Bond production designers including Sir Ken Adam, Syd Cain, Peter Murton and Peter Lamont. They, along with Allan Cameron and Dennis Gassner, have established and developed the look of the movies. Undoubtedly the greatest influence has been that of Ken Adam – his sloping roofs, gigantic sets and wonderful blending of the futuristic and classic was revolutionary. On *Goldfinger*, his fictionalized vision of the interior of Fort Knox caused the American authorities to question their obvious breach of security – even they thought it was real.

Ken also changed the face of Pinewood's lot for ever when he designed and built the huge 007 Stage. He and Cubby scoured the country looking for a facility big enough to house three nuclear submarines. They couldn't find anything, so Cubby said, 'Build it.'

In 1984, just prior to our commencing work on *A View To A Kill*, word came through that the 007 Stage was on fire. But how can a huge steel structure catch fire? It turned out that Tom Cruise's film *Legend* was shooting on there and, during a lunch break, a gas canister exploded. Within minutes, the stage interior was alight and effectively melted.

Cubby later visited the site with production designer Peter Lamont and asked, 'How long and how much to rebuild?' Peter

gave him an answer of sixteen weeks and £1 million. Cubby said, 'OK, do it.' The stage was re-opened and renamed the 'Albert R. Broccoli 007 Stage', in honour of Cubby.

Tragically, on 30 July 2006 during my Sunday lunch, I received a call to say 'Pinewood is on fire'. I dropped my roast parsnips and made a few calls. It turned out to be the 007 Stage (again). During the set dismantling of *Casino Royale*, a blowtorch pilot light was left burning and – over the course of the weekend – a fire broke out and crept towards some gas bottles. In a matter of hours a black, molten mess was all that remained. Six months later, the third incarnation of our stage was opened.

LET THERE BE MUSIC

Another hugely important element of the films is, of course, the music. While Monty Norman wrote the 'James Bond theme', it was really through the efforts of a Yorkshireman by the name of John Barry that its orchestration became the most famous theme music in the world – which still greets me from pianists when I walk into restaurants or hotel bars. Do I mind? Of course not.

John scored eleven of the films, of which four were mine. He was a lovely, intelligent and gentle man, though one who didn't suffer fools in his work. Unfortunately, John suffered a ruptured oesophagus in 1988, following a toxic reaction to a health tonic he consumed, and was unable to tackle his twelfth Bond score for *Licence To Kill*. In fact, he couldn't work for a couple years. When *GoldenEye* came around, different people had different ideas about the music and they didn't coincide with John's thinking. He departed the franchise, but subsequently handed over the baton to a pair of very safe hands in David Arnold.

From my own films, I think the best Bond theme is 'Nobody Does It Better', as performed by Carly Simon. It sums up Jim brilliantly. It might not have charted as high as one or two others, but it's probably (now) the most played Bond song on radio, and to my mind is in the true style of brash, bold and melodic Bond fanfares – you left the cinema humming it. Can that be said of more recent title songs, I wonder?

Going hand in hand with the wonderful title music are the opening titles, and for so very many years they were designed by Maurice Binder, who also created the legendary gun barrel opening sequence that produces goosebumps on the back of all Bond fans'

DIRECTORS ABOVE FROM TOP:
Dennis Gassner has designed the sets for the last two Daniel Craig films. Here he is in conversation with director Marc Forster.

Here with Michael Wilson and Barbara Broccoli is the director of *Tomorrow Never Dies,* Roger Spottiswoode.

OPPOSITE FROM TOP:
Martin Campbell has directed two in the series so far. Let's hope he returns for the hat trick.

Guy Hamilton was in charge of four Bond films, including two of mine.

Lee Tamahori perhaps directed the most outlandish of all, *Die Another Day.*

John Glen served as second unit diretor, editor and then became director, helming five 007 films, three of which were mine. Thanks, John.

ABOVE: Maurice Binder taught me how to fire right down the barrel of his lens. He created the famous gun barrel opening for the Bond films, and also designed so many of the wonderful opening titles.

BELOW: Long-time Bond composer John Barry with his wife Laurie at the *Licence To Kill* premiere. Sadly ill health had prevented him from scoring the movie.

necks, and I do hope it returns proper with Daniel Craig's third outing.

As the sequence was only ever intended to show Bond in silhouette, Sean Connery's double Bob Simmons was used to film the opening to *Dr. No*. The sequence was used in the next couple of films, but for *Thunderball* – which used the Panavision anamorphic format – it had to be re-shot, and this time they brought Sean in.

I filmed it twice myself: my first two films were shot in 1.85:1 whereas for *Spy* they reverted to the anamorphic format. I know a bit about lenses, having been a director, you see. Not just a pretty face!

Maurice was a perfectionist, and that wasn't without problems. You see, long after we'd wrapped and the release date was announced, he'd be hard at work. As the premiere approached and our PR machine cranked up, he'd still be hard at work. The film was then, and finally, submitted to the BBFC for certification, and Maurice was still hard at work! I often said the titles were still wet when they left Maurice's studio – usually the night before the premiere. But Maurice would never let anyone interfere, and I think that's why he always delivered at the last minute – so nobody had the time to.

He was such a kindly man, and I remember being in LA for his memorial service a couple of months after he died in 1991. Harry's son, Chris Saltzman, spoke with huge fondness of the man who was their Father Christmas. Every year, Harry would ask his slightly rotund friend to don the outfit and play Santa for the children, and every year Maurice did.

M

Bernard Lee – Bernie – played M in eleven of the Bond films. He was asked to appear in *For Your Eyes Only* but his health was waning, and he declined. Cubby pleaded with him to reconsider, and Bernie said, 'I'll come in and test for you,' wanting to prove his point. Sadly, he was very weak, stumbled over his lines and simply couldn't finish the scene. Cubby reluctantly agreed to let his friend stand down, though insisted the part would not be recast immediately. Shortly afterwards, Bernie passed away. A couple of his scenes in the film were given to Desmond Llewelyn, and James Villiers took the others as Chief of Staff, in M's place, saying his boss was on leave.

I had worked with Bernie Lee on a couple of earlier occasions – *Crossplot* and *The Persuaders!* – but very nearly didn't get to work with him on my debut *Live And Let Die* as, just before filming commenced, his wife Gladys tragically died in a house fire. Uncertain as to whether Bernie would be able to reprise his role, the producers suggested I ask Kenneth More if he would be prepared to step in. Kenneth agreed that he could be available on condition his fee be sent to Bernie.

Bernie insisted that he would return, and we filmed our scenes on B-stage at Pinewood, which was dressed as Bond's flat; the only time, I believe, apart from in *Dr. No* that we ever saw Jim's abode, which scholars believe to be in Wellington Square, Chelsea.

Geoffrey Keen was cast as the Defence Minister in *The Spy Who Loved Me* and stayed for five more films. He actually became a bit of a minder to Bernie Lee, particularly when we were on location in Venice filming *Moonraker*. Bernie had a tendency to disappear to a bar, and dear Geoffrey had to keep him out!

When *Octopussy* was gearing up and the question of finding a new M arose, Cubby asked me what I thought. I suggested he might call in Robert Brown for a chat. Bob and I worked on *Ivanhoe* together and I thought he'd be very good as the stoic M. Cubby obviously agreed. Sean, meanwhile, was busy making *Never Say Never Again*, and cast Edward Fox as M.

Of course, in 1995, when Bond returned after the hiatus, the world had changed and Stella Rimmington was head of MI6, prompting the casting of a female M. Who else but the superb Dame Judi Dench?

PULLING STUNTS

Behind every successful action hero lies a talented stunt team. Looking at the closing titles of a Bond film, you might count a hundred or more such folks – from drivers, aerial specialists, skiers, acrobats, horse riders ... and sex doubles. Well, would you expect me to get into bed with Grace Jones?

When I was in *The Saint* and *The Persuaders!* Les Crawford was my brave double. He came with me for the first two Bonds, but then Martin Grace took on the role. Martin became a great friend, and I always enjoyed hanging around with him and the other stunt boys off set, playing cards, chewing the fat and exchanging funny stories.

Martin was terribly brave. He'd think nothing of hanging off the side of a helicopter, a steep cliff, or even a moving train. Sadly, on *Octopussy*, he was doing the latter when the fast moving engine took the train beyond a checked stretch of line at the Nene Valley Railway (doubling for East Germany) and Martin hit a concrete post. He gripped onto the train, refusing to fall and risk going under, but sustained terrible injuries. He was in hospital for months and it was feared he might never walk again, let alone return to work. But such was the stamina of the man that on my next film, *A View To A Kill*, he was back on set.

One of the most talked-about stunts of any Bond film was performed by Rick Sylvester. I am, of course, referring to the pre-title ski-jump in *The Spy Who Loved Me*. I remember the premiere so vividly, when a total hush descended over the auditorium as he, playing me, skied off that perpendicular cliff. The silence was broken by amazing applause when the Union Flag parachute opened. The idea came to Cubby after seeing a magazine advertisement of a similar jump, made by Rick. It was one of the riskiest and most costly sequences ever imagined and if there was ever any doubt in Cubby Broccoli's mind that his first Bond film as a solo producer was going to be anything other than a huge hit, that moment reassured everyone involved.

SAY CHEESE

I must mention my friends in the camera department who made me look so very beautiful on the big screen. Long-time lighting cameraman Ted Moore was on the very first Bond, and worked on my first two before ill health caused him to withdraw from *The Man With The Golden Gun*, and Ossie Morris replaced him. Two very talented Frenchmen, Claude Renoir and Jean Tournier joined Lewis Gilbert and me, before Alan Hume was given the opportunity to lens *For Your Eyes Only*, *Octopussy* and *A View To A Kill* with my old mate from *The Saint* Alec Mills as his operator. I used to tease young Alec relentlessly, and I remember when we were working on *The Spy Who Loved Me* Lewis suggested it would be an idea to film the inside of a submarine missile tube, to give the impression of a missile loading. Alec refused, unless he was given a guarantee I was not on board. He reckoned I'd hit the 'fire' button. Me? Would I?!

We were on location somewhere or other and I remember Alec coming down for breakfast in the hotel, looking rather ashen faced. He explained that half way through the night his door opened and a big burly guy came in and climbed into bed with him and fell asleep. Alec said, in a state of semi-sleep, he was quite terrified.

Elaine Shreyeck, our wonderful continuity supervisor, asked 'Was he tight? [meaning drunk]'

I couldn't help myself, and called out, 'Only the first time!'

Alan and Alec took great trouble to make the leading ladies look good, and as a result made me look less pretty. But I don't bear a grudge.

ABOVE LEFT: Special-effects pioneer John Stears (centre), with his right hand men Burt Luxford (left) and Joe Fitt, was one of only two people to ever win an Oscar for a Bond film.

ABOVE RIGHT: Alec Mills on set with Cubby Broccoli, probably complaining he couldn't see me and wanted to know where I was as he never trusted me outside his eye line!

FAR LEFT: A brave bunch of boys made me look so good on screen – be it hanging from a helicopter or skiing off a mountain.

BELOW LEFT: Here is my stunt dream team: George Leech, Paul Weston, Martin Grace, Richard Graydon.

BOND
ON
SCREEN

PREVIOUS PAGES: Daniel Craig
was presented to Her Majesty
at the premiere of *Casino
Royale* in 2006.

TOP RIGHT: *From Russia With
Love* didn't have a premiere,
but its opening was big news.

RIGHT: Cover stories – being
Jim Bond could never be
described as a low-key
occupation.

BELOW: Sean gets in the
swing of things during the
Thunderball post-premiere
party.

BOND ON SCREEN

A vital part of making any Bond film is promotion, publicity and premieres. It's all very well having made a film, but people need to know about it and want to go and see it; only then will its success be judged at the box office. Personally, I don't like to bring up the subject of money, but you can find the budgets and worldwide gross takings of each film towards the back of the book – it makes for interesting reading.

CAUGHT IN THE WEB

There is always a huge press and public interest when a new Bond film is announced. At the time of writing, for example, Daniel Craig's third 007 adventure, *Skyfall*, is in pre-production just a few doors down the corridor from my office at Pinewood Studios. The Art Department has all manner of sketches, models and storyboards laid out; the runner's office is bursting with mail, coffee machines and baskets of fruit and snacks; the executives, accountants and producers are ensconced in suites a few doors further along and everybody who walks down the corridor is fascinated by the names on the doors and asks, 'So what's this one about?'

During my tenure as Bond, there was no such thing as the Internet. Any titbits of information and production stills were released to the media through the Unit Publicist's office, and they'd appear as 'exclusives' in newspapers and magazines around the world, all slowly building to a bigger and bigger deluge as premiere time approached, when United Artists swung its entire marketing team behind us. Back then, the various fan club publications carried the odd rumour, early photographs and potential storylines. Now all of that is on the Web, with daily updates and interactive forums where anybody can post just about anything – and they are no doubt frustrated by the huge secrecy surrounding a production. Well, if you were spending $100 million+ the last thing you'd want is everybody to know everything about a film before you even make it.

By the way, everyone – but everyone – on the film is sworn to secrecy and has to sign a confidentiality agreement. Scripts are kept under lock and key and all are watermarked. But let me tell you all you need to know: it's going to be a great film, with lots of action, wonderful gadgets and rather beautiful leading ladies – the rest is to be discovered and enjoyed in a darkened room with 350 of your local neighbours.

TALKING THE TALK

Product placement and tie-ins have always been a big part of the 007 movies. Sean promoted Smirnoff Vodka way back in *Dr. No* and mentioned a certain brand of champagne too. That wasn't just by chance – that was paid for by the manufacturer. Bond tie-ins over the years have featured everything from the drinks, watches and cars I've written about elsewhere in this book, to things like airlines (Richard Branson's Virgin), toys, clocks, soft drinks – Coke, 7Up, Perrier – Easter eggs, sweets, stickers, dolls, stationery, mugs, T-shirts, lighters and so very much more. I haven't been surprised to see my face on ties or underpants either.

The exploitation of Bond is really all controlled by Eon, Danjaq and their marketing departments, as once run by Jerry Juroe, John Parkinson and Anne Bennett, and now Keith Snelgrove and Stephanie Wenborn. I am fortunate in that a few pennies occasionally find their way to me from my little involvement. It keeps an old actor in baked beans, y'know.

Ahead of any premiere, out-of-town journalists converge on London for a press junket. United Artists would take four or five rooms at one of the big hotels, set up TV cameras and wheel in the TV journalists one by one. I'd be in situ and they'd get a few minutes with me, before being given a tape of what we'd just recorded, and waved goodbye. This would go on all morning, then they'd call lunch … and I'd move into a dining room full of tables of twelve print journalists, all waiting to interview me. I'd spend three or four hours, shifting between tables while trying to eat the odd mouthful of food. It was always quite an exhausting couple of days – and one that was repeated in each major city we visited overseas.

Then there are the film festivals, the most famous and important of which is Cannes each May. There Jimmy usually graces the front of the Carlton Hotel on La Croisette. I must admit, when promoting *The Spy Who Loved Me*, it was rather intimidating to drive up and see my face all over the famous building. Okay, I admit there is a fizzy thrill the first time you see it, but after that passes, it becomes a little embarrassing. As a rule I always try to avoid festivals, as they're simply too terrifying for modest actors such as I.

As for the previews and premieres, I could have quite probably seen any one of my Bond films twenty times over. Imagine having to endure that! After the Royal premiere, where, of course, I sat with the Royal Party, I'd then avoid sitting through the film again. Sure, I'd walk the red carpet of whatever city we were premiering in, but then Cubby and I would sneak out and head off for dinner.

These premieres are always very glamorous occasions, where the stars and principals of the movie, plus a few other stars from TV and film, come together to unveil the movie to world audiences.

ABOVE LEFT: I'm never late for an audition, thanks to my trusted Zeon alarm clock.

ABOVE RIGHT: A few of these gold-plated Lotus Esprit models were made for presentation to the Royal party, stars and a few other folks during the premiere of *The Spy Who Loved Me*.

ABOVE: Another close shave averted!

THE PREMIERE EVENT

Although the first two Bond films were just screened at the Pavilion Cinemas in Piccadilly Circus, from *Goldfinger* onwards there were premieres, usually at the Odeon Leicester Square. With its 2,000 seats (now reduced to 1,683), it really is the cathedral of British cinema, and helps launch each film with style, excitement and fanfare.

On the evening of the *Goldfinger* premiere, 5,000 fans gathered outside the Odeon Leicester Square to watch the cans of film being delivered by armoured truck, but little did they know that Guy Hamilton was still shooting the final scenes in those cans in America just a few days earlier.

'The first thing to be locked on any Bond film is the premiere,' Guy told me. 'And that date is set in stone – you have to hit it. No excuses.'

Sean didn't attend the opening, as he was in Spain shooting *The Hill*. However, all his co-stars were there, including Honor Blackman, who wore a diamond ring worth £10,000.

ABOVE: Paul and Linda McCartney, who sang the theme tune, attending the premiere of *Live And Let Die*.

LEFT: As did I and Jane Seymour, where we were presented to Her Majesty The Queen Mother. Jean-Pierre Cassel (with whom I was filming *That Lucky Touch*), looks on.

ABOVE AND BELOW:
A miniature Bonding session.
And a fan magazine.

When *Thunderball* premiered in December 1965 at the Hibiya Cinema in Tokyo, Japan had become the epicentre of Bondmania and old Jim was dubbed 'Mr Kiss Kiss Bang Bang'. How appropriate.

At the New York premiere a few days later, United Artists arranged for one of the Bell Jet-Pack pilots to fly off the marquee of the Paramount Theatre at 1501 Broadway, Manhattan, as a promotion at the launch. A number of United Artists publicity personnel and the pilot were arrested as no one had sought permission from the authorities. The UK hosted dual premieres in London on 29 December 1965 at the Rialto Theatre and Pavilion Theatre, Piccadilly Circus.

You Only Live Twice premiered on 12 June 1967 at the Odeon Leicester Square, and marked Sean's first attendance at a Bond opening since *From Russia With Love*. The unofficial spoof version of *Casino Royale* also opened the same year, and United Artists pulled out all the stops to ensure *You Only Live Twice* scored bigger at the box office, and insisted that posters read Sean Connery IS James Bond.

To mark the event, two television specials were broadcast. The first, on BBC1 in the UK, was a special edition of *Whicker's World* with a behind-the-scenes look at the film. NBC in the USA meanwhile broadcast *Welcome To Japan, Mr Bond*, featuring skits by M, Q and Moneypenny.

The premiere was graced by the appearance of Her Majesty Queen Elizabeth II and her husband Prince Philip – their first James Bond premiere – and it broke the opening-day record at the Odeon and instantly became the number one film in the USA when it opened there the following day.

By the premiere of *On Her Majesty's Secret Service* in December 1969, the new 007, George Lazenby, had already decided to quit when he attended the event. Against the wishes of the producers,

he arrived sporting long hair and a bushy beard, looking nothing like his on-screen persona. Although profits were down compared with earlier films, *On Her Majesty's Secret Service* has since been regarded by critics and fans as one of the best Bond films, outside of my own, of course.

Diamonds Are Forever premiered on 17 December 1971 at the DeMille Theatre in New York, followed by a British premiere on 30 December at the Odeon Leicester Square, London. The film broke records again at the Odeon, taking £35,000 in its first week (£13,500 more than the previous high).

Unlike *On Her Majesty's Secret Service*, which overshot by two months, principal photography on *Diamonds Are Forever* wrapped on Friday, 13 August, bang on time, and no doubt in part due to Sean's contract adding an additional $145,000 on top of his salary of $1.25 million for every week the production overran.

ABOVE: Although there was no premiere for *Dr. No*, the first-night opening was attended by cast and crew at the London Pavilion followed by a dinner. Sean was accompanied by Zena Marshall.

NERVOUS, JIMMY?

I can honestly say that the only time I was nervous about being the new James Bond was on the way to the premiere of *Live And Let Die*. We'd been shooting for months, I'd attended countless press conferences and interviews, but in the car on the way to the Odeon Leicester Square on 5 July 1973, the labour pains started. 'The baby is coming out and it's too late to do anything about it,' I told myself.

HRH Princess Anne graced the event, and thankfully the audience didn't all get up and walk out halfway through. They asked me back for a second film, so all was not lost.

The Man With The Golden Gun premiered on 18 December 1974, at the Odeon Leicester Square in the presence of HRH Prince Philip.

Incidentally, this was the first James Bond movie to be shown at the Kremlin. When the movie had finished, one Russian official

LEFT: Director Guy Hamilton and his wife Keri are presented to HRH the Duke of Edinburgh in the Royal line up at the Odeon Leicester Square for *The Man With The Golden Gun*.

ABOVE: *For Your Eyes Only*
was HRH Princess Diana's
first Royal Premiere, which
she attended with HRH
Prince Charles and HRH
Princess Margaret.

turned around to Cubby and said, 'We didn't train Scaramanga very well, did we?'

The Spy Who Loved Me premiered on 7 July 1977. The date on the posters read 07/07/77. Jim's lucky numbers. This was Cubby's first solo Bond production, and he was obviously anxious it was a success. After Rick Sylvester (doubling for me in the ski stunt) launched himself off the snowy cliff top to reveal a Union Jack parachute, the audience leapt to their feet and cheered – and Cubby smiled widely. 007 was back!

A limited number of gold Lotus Esprit models were produced for the evening, and presented to the Royal Party, myself and one or two other notables.

The post-premiere party was held at the InterContinental Hotel in Park Lane and cost £143,000 – the budget of a small British film.

When *Moonraker* premiered, the original plan was to do it in

Houston, to coincide with the first launch of NASA's new space shuttle. However, the space shuttle was delayed for two years, and we returned to the Odeon Leicester Square on 26 June 1979 instead.

A large model Moonraker space shuttle was driven around the square, accompanied by two extras in space suits and greeting celebrity guests including Richard Kiel, Michael Lonsdale, Corinne Clery, Blanche Ravalec, Bernard Lee, Toshiro Suga, former Bond girl Britt Ekland, along with big names of the day Joan Collins, Dodi Fayed, Dino De Laurentis, Michael Winner and Richard Johnson.

A post-premiere party was held at the London Playboy Club with the bunny girls dressed in space outfits. The Odeon took £86,084 in its first week, breaking records once again.

For Your Eyes Only premiered on 24 June 1981 at the Odeon Leicester Square in the presence of Prince Charles and (the then) Lady Diana Spencer. It was the first ever premiere they'd attended together, and my daughter Deborah was asked to travel to Kensington Palace to meet and escort them. Thousands of fans waited hours for the Royal couple, who were also accompanied by Princess Margaret.

I presented the Prince of Wales with a solid-gold version of a 007 Seiko digital watch, which played the James Bond theme at the touch of a button.

I then sat next to Lady Diana during the screening and, being conscious of having had a Jack Daniel's or two in the run-up to the evening, I acquired a little spray to freshen my breath, and kept it in my hand throughout. Apparently, this amused Diana, as she reported back to the Palace that I must have thought my halitosis would bother her.

Topol, who played Columbo in the film, suggested to Cubby he should invite his former producing partner Harry Saltzman to the event. Their split had been acrimonious, but time is a great healer and the reunion was a happy one.

Unbeknown to us all, there was also a future James Bond in the audience that night, as Pierce Brosnan accompanied his wife Cassandra Harris.

Their Royal Highnesses the Prince and Princess of Wales joined us once again for the premiere of *Octopussy* on 6 June 1981 at the Odeon Leicester Square. By this time, United Artists had all but collapsed after

ABOVE: The *Moonraker* post-premiere party was at the Playboy Club in Park Lane.

BELOW: Richard Kiel is presented to HRH Princess Anne.

ABOVE: Marvel produced this *Octopussy* special annual.

TOP RIGHT: Diana Rigg and George Lazenby at the *On Her Majesty's Secret Service* premiere at the Odeon Leicester Square. Cubby and Harry were not best pleased when their star turned up with a beard and long hair, looking quite unlike his screen image.

BOTTOM RIGHT: Pierce Brosnan and Halle Berry at the Royal Albert Hall for *Die Another Day*.

the disastrous financial problems *Heaven's Gate* had left in its wake. However, MGM structured a merger/buy-out deal and swung behind the thirteenth Bond adventure (particularly with Sean's unofficial *Never Say Never Again* lurking on the release schedule) with a huge marketing campaign.

Never Say Never Again premiered on 7 October 1983 in the USA, before a Royal Premiere on 14 December at the Warner West End cinema in the presence of HRH Prince Andrew. The film drew largely positive reviews, though the lack of familiar 007 elements such as the music, gun barrel opening and MI6 staff disappointed some fans. Originally, Peter Hunt had been offered the chance to direct, though declined, as did Richard Donner. Irvin Kershner ultimately took the helm. Incidentally, MGM acquired the distribution rights to the movie in 1997 after its acquisition of Orion Pictures.

I never saw it myself. I probably never will. But, then again, never say never, eh?

It was San Francisco's Palace of Fine Arts that welcomed the world premiere of *A View To A Kill* in May 1985. Given the overwhelming cooperation the city had offered us during filming, Cubby decided they should benefit from hosting the event. It was followed a few weeks later with a UK premiere, on 12 June, at the Odeon Leicester Square in the presence of TRH The Prince and Princess of Wales.

Of course, all the press asked me if I'd do another Bond, to which I replied, 'I wouldn't be a bit surprised.' I knew I wouldn't do any more, but the last thing you do at a film opening is announce you're retiring!

THE NEW BOYS

By the time the premiere of *The Living Daylights* rolled around in June 1987, Timothy Dalton's debut opened to positive press and a healthy box office and people were saying, 'Roger who?'

Pierce Brosnan's debut film *GoldenEye* launched in New York City on 17 November 1995. Five days later, on 22 November, in the presence of HRH the Prince of Wales, it premiered at the Odeon Leicester Square. After a six-year absence from the screen, the newspapers declared 007 was well and truly back. The movie smashed records, and overtook *Moonraker* in the box-office stakes.

After my retirement I purposely avoided attending any of the premieres, though I did attend the premiere for *Die Another Day*

ACKNOWLEDGMENTS

The James Bond films, and images
from which, are (c) 1962-2012
Danjaq LLC and United Artists Corp,
All Rights Reserved.

I am extremely grateful to the
following people for helping
make this book a reality: Barbara
Broccoli, Michael Wilson, Meg
Simmonds and Darren Bailey
of EON Productions Ltd; Dave
Worrall and Lee Pfeiffer of www.
cinemaretro.com; Andrew Boyle
of Bondstars.com; Doris Spriggs;
John Willis; Audie Charles of
Haywards; Paul Weston (Stunts);
Iris (Eagle-eye) Harwood; Lesley
Pollinger of Pollinger Ltd; Mike and
Lesley O'Mara; Louise Dixon, Ana
Bjezancevic and George Maudsley
of Michael O'Mara Books; Andy
Armitage; Ron Callow of Design
23; and Gareth Owen, for his
ghostly assistance, encyclopaedic
knowledge and for always
answering the phone.

For photographs I am indebted to:
Harry Myers; David Zaritsky; Joseph
Darlington www.beingjamesbond.
com; Ed Maggiani at TheSpyBoys.
com; George Vasquez; Rick Dos
Santos; Barry Koper; Tony Harwood;
Pete Harrison; Robin Harbour – the
West Midlands' biggest collector
of James Bond memorabilia; Robin
Morgan and Terry O'Neill for the
Doug Hayward photo; Martjin
Mulder / On the Tracks of 007
http://dmd-digital.nl/